MW01143856

5-Minute Devotions
for Youth Ministry

Loveland, Colorado

Group's R.E.A.L. Guarantee to you:

This Group resource incorporates our R.E.A.L. approach to ministry—one that encourages long-term retention and life transformation. It's ministry that's:

Relational
Because learner-to-learner interaction enhances learning and builds Christian friendships.

Experiential
Because what learners experience through discussion and action sticks with them up to 9 times longer than what they simply hear or read.

Applicable
Because the aim of Christian education is to equip learners to be both hearers and doers of God's Word.

Learner-based
Because learners understand and retain more when the learning process takes into consideration how they learn best.

5-Minute Devotions
for Youth Ministry

Copyright © 2003 Group Publishing, Inc.

Visit our Web site: **www.grouppublishing.com**

Credits
Contributing Authors: Jenny Baker, Rick Beno, Bristow Hood, Mikal Keefer, James W. Miller, Julia L. Roller, Kate Sabott, Christina Schofield, Alison Simpson, and Helen Turnbull
Editor: Kelli B. Trujillo
Creative Development Editor: Amy Simpson
Chief Creative Officer: Joani Schultz
Copy Editor: Lyndsay E. Gerwing
Art Director: Kari K. Monson
Cover Designer: Blukazoo Studio
Print Production Artist: Joyce Douglas
Illustrator: Jennifer Kalis
Production Manager: Dodie Tipton

Unless otherwise noted, Scripture taken from the HOLY BIBLE, NEW INTERNATIONAL VERSION®. Copyright © 1973, 1978, 1984 by International Bible Society. Used by permission of Zondervan Publishing House. All rights reserved.

Library of Congress Cataloging-in-Publication Data
5-minute devotions for youth ministry.
    p. cm.
Includes indexes.
ISBN 0-7644-2421-1 (alk. paper)
1. Church work with youth. I. Group Publishing. II. Title:
Five-minute devotions for youth ministry.
BV4447 .A13 2002
259'.23--dc21
    2002007654

10 9 8 7 6 5 4 3   12 11 10 09 08 07 06 05

Printed in the United States of America.

Contents

Introduction

Are you...

• preparing for a Bible study and trying to think of a creative way to get discussion started?

• planning a party or trip and wondering if there's a way to add a spiritual dimension to the event?

• in need of a quick and easy low-prep idea for a "last-minute" youth meeting?

• looking for ideas you can customize to build your own lesson and meet your ministry's specific needs?

If you've ever been in any of these situations, then *5-Minute Devotions for Youth Ministry* is the right place to look. These 100 short devotion ideas cover the topics you're teaching, such as courage, alcohol and drugs, divorce, faith, idolatry, loneliness, materialism, and 93 more! Each devotion idea highlights a specific Scripture passage and includes several discussion questions to help teenagers dig deep into biblical truth.

The great thing about these devotions is that they're full of variety! *5-Minute Devotions* includes:

• *Activity Devotions*—creative games, team-building challenges, and interactive discussion starters;

• *Event and Location Devotions*—ideas for using youth ministry events or unique locations to creatively inspire life change;

• *Illustration Devotions*—fictional and real-life stories on critical topics;

• *Movie and Music Devotions*—specific video clip and song suggestions to help you use pop culture to provoke discussion; and

• *Object-Lesson Devotions*—inventive ideas for using everyday objects to explore Bible truths.

To use this book, simply flip to the section that contains the type of devotion you're looking for, read "The Scoop" on that section, and then get started. Or use the indexes on pages 103-109 to find the devotion that fits just what you're lookin' for. The indexes will help you find devotions according to topic, Scripture passage, event, location, movie, or song.

So if you only have five minutes—or if you plan on transforming one of these ideas into a full-blown Bible study—*5-Minute Devotions for Youth Ministry* will meet your ministry needs. Have fun as you creatively use and adapt these *5-Minute Devotions* to inspire spiritual growth in teenagers' lives!

Activity Devotions

ere's where you'll find games, creative projects, imagination exercises, team challenges, and other interesting activities to get teenagers exploring Scripture and discussing important issues. Each of these activities takes about five minutes. After the activity, use one or two discussion questions or the whole bunch to dive into a full-fledged exploration of the topic.

Topic: The Church

Living Stones

Scripture Focus: 1 Peter 2:4-10

Supplies: Bibles, 5 matches for each student, poster tack

The Activity

Give everyone a small blob of poster tack and five matches, and say: **I want you to use what I've given you to make a church.**

Don't give students any other instructions. Most people will assume that this is an exercise about working together and will pool their resources to try to make a church building together. However, they can also each make a person from their materials—one matchstick for the body, two for the arms, two for the legs, and the poster tack to make a head and to hold it all together. Allow students some time to work, then ask teenagers to explain what they've created. If none of the students have made a person out of their supplies, make one yourself and show it to students, explaining that it also fits the definition of *church*.

Discussion

• **Why did you decide to make what you did?**

Read 1 Peter 2:4-10.

• **What does Jesus call us at the beginning of this passage? What are we being built into? Explain.**

• **Most people think of a building when they hear the word *church*, but what else can the word refer to?**

• **What's the significance of the church being people rather than a building?**

• **This Scripture says each stone is precious. What contribution can you make to the life of the church?**

Topic: Doubt

I Think I Can, I Think I Can...

Scripture Focus: Matthew 14:22-36

Supplies: Bibles, stopwatch

The Activity

Ask students to form trios, and tell them that you're going to give them a challenge. In the trios, each person must talk as quickly as he or she can for forty-five seconds about one of the following subjects: least favorite subject in school, how his or her two best friends are alike and different, or why his or her favorite movie is so good. Here's the catch: The students absolutely *cannot* use "uh," "ah," "um," or "like" during their monologues! After you have announced the beginning and end of each forty-five-second segment (don't forget to keep track of the time!), gather the students back together.

Discussion

• Beforehand, did you think you could talk without stopping and without using the "forbidden" words? Why or why not?

• If you doubted you could, what did you do differently than usual as you talked?

Read Matthew 14:22-36.

• What happened when Peter began to doubt?

• What things do you have doubts about?

• Why are Jesus' words in this passage important? How can they help you overcome doubt?

Topic: Failure

Jesus' Report Card

Scripture Focus: Romans 3:21-24

Supplies: Bibles, 2 copies of the "Report Card" handout (p. 10) for each student, pens

The Activity

Make enough photocopies of the "Report Card" handout on page 10 so that each student can have two copies. Distribute a handout and a pen to each student, and have students write their names at the top and fill in the grades they think they've earned in the specified "subjects." Next, give each student a second copy, and ask students to write Jesus' name at the top, filling in all A's for the subjects. Finally, have students use pens to switch the names on the two report cards, giving themselves Jesus' grades.

Discussion

• Do you deserve these new grades? Why or why not?

• What does it feel like to recognize your own failures?

• How did Jesus "switch report cards" with us when he died on the cross?

Read Romans 3:21-24.

• What does it mean to be justified? Explain.

• How can switching report cards affect your perspective on your own failures?

Report Card

Name: _____

Subjects	Grades
Moral Behavior	_____
Good Works	_____
Generosity	_____
Clean Speech	_____
Pure Thoughts	_____
Helpfulness	_____
Kindness	_____

Topic: Fasting

Distractions, Distractions

Scripture Focus: Matthew 6:16-18

Supplies: Bibles

The Activity

Ask your students to demonstrate how they can snap their fingers. If some students absolutely can't do it—with either hand—have them open and close each hand rapidly, smacking their thumbs against other fingers to make noise.

Say: **Please continue to snap your fingers right next to your own ears, as rapidly and loudly as possible, until I raise a hand to signal that you should stop.**

Once students are snapping, say the following, being careful to speak softly enough that it's difficult for students to hear you over the sound of the snapping.

Say: **Here's important information for you. Listen carefully, and do exactly as I tell you.**

Then explain how your group should evacuate the building in case of fire. When you've finished, signal that students should quit snapping. Repeat the information.

Discussion

- **How easy or difficult was it for you to hear me while you were distracted by finger snapping? Why?**
- **What things in your daily lives distract you from completing schoolwork in the best possible way?**
- **What things in your daily lives distract you from living out your Christian faith in the best possible way?**

Read Matthew 6:16-18.

- **According to Jesus' words, does fasting appear to be an important part of Christian devotion? Why or why not?**
- **Fasting is one way to sacrifice the distraction of appetite for a time in order to focus on God. What could happen if you set aside a mealtime and used it for prayer rather than for eating?**

Topic: Following God's Plan

Aerobicize!

Scripture Focus: John 5:19

Supplies: Bibles, stopwatch

The Activity

Have students form pairs, and designate a leader and a follower in each pair. Explain that the leader should take five seconds to do several motions (such as a jumping jack, a muscle flex, and three claps). The follower will watch the motions and will then try to replicate them exactly, in the correct order. Use the stopwatch to call time between five-second rounds. Encourage students to take turns leading and following. If some pairs are doing a good job following each other, prompt them to do motions for ten or twenty seconds for an extra challenge.

Discussion

• **What did you have to do in order to accomplish your job as follower?**

• **How is following God different from trying to follow your partner in this exercise? How is it similar?**

• **Is it easy or hard to follow God's plan for your life? Explain.**

Read John 5:19.

• **How did Jesus follow God? How is this similar to the activity we just did?**

• **How will you watch for what God is doing and then follow him this week?**

Topic: God's Voice

Can You Hear Me?

Practice Makes Perfect!

Take some time to master this activity before you try it with students so that you can demonstrate how it works.

Scripture Focus: 1 Kings 19:11-13

Supplies: Bibles, 2 empty paper cups for each student

The Activity

Give each student two empty paper cups. Ask students to drop the first cup inside the second cup, letting the first nest loosely inside the second.

Say: **Here's the challenge: to get the top cup out of the bottom one without turning the cups over and without** touching the top cup. **Start by shouting at your cups to see if you can vibrate the first cup out. Use different tones and volumes.**

Let students try this for a few seconds. The approach will fail. Then show students how to blow across the lips of the cups. The first cup nested inside the second cup will lift and float upward and out.

Discussion

• **Shouting at the cup didn't get the desired response. Does shouting at you motivate you to do things? Why or why not?**

• **If you could hear God's voice, how do you think it would sound? Describe it.** Read 1 Kings 19:11-13.

• **What does this tell you about God's voice? about God's power and how God uses it?**

• **How was your yelling at the cups and then quietly blowing across the cups like God speaking to Elijah?**

• **How can you listen to God's voice this week?**

Topic: Hunger for God

Single-Minded, Single-Hearted

Scripture Focus: Psalm 42:1-2

Supplies: Bibles

The Activity

Ask students to find a comfortable place to sit and to close their eyes. Assure them that no one will touch them.

Say the following, adding ten-second pauses as indicated so that students have time to focus and imagine.

Say: **Picture a wide, white, sandy beach.** Pause. **The sun is warm, the sky is a brilliant blue, and the beach is empty.** Pause. **Sea gulls wheel and turn overhead.** Pause. **Palm trees sway behind you.** Pause. **Waves break out away from shore. Picture the cool, turquoise water gently reaching up onto the beach and then rolling back. You feel the sand between your toes as you stroll.** Pause. **This is the ultimate**

vacation. You're content. Pause. **You're happy.** Pause. **You wish you could be here, relaxed and satisfied, forever.**

Read through the script again, but this second time, challenge students to hold their breath as you read.

Discussion

• **How were your two imaginary vacations alike? different?**

• **When you were holding your breath, how difficult or easy was it for you to keep your focus on the images I was asking you to imagine? Why?**

Read Psalm 42:1-2.

• **During our activity, our physical hunger for oxygen took center stage when we weren't getting it. What would your life be like if your hunger for God had the same urgency and immediacy?**

• **How can you increase your own spiritual hunger for God?**

Topic: Loving Others

A Loving Litany

Scripture Focus: 1 John 3:16-18

Supplies: Bibles, index cards, hat, pens

The Activity

Distribute an index card and pen to each student, and ask students to write a brief summary of one experience they've had with seeing or knowing of someone in need. For example, a student may have seen a homeless man walking in the cold with no coat or may have a friend who is a single parent.

Put all the cards in a hat, and have each student draw a different card. Ask students to each think of one way they could meet the needs on their cards. Encourage them to take turns using their ideas to complete the following sentence aloud: "Loving is..." For example, a student could say, "Loving is seeing a homeless man walking in the cold with no coat, and taking your coat off and giving it to him."

Discussion

• **Have you ever had someone tell you that he or she loves you but then do something mean or hurtful to you? Describe that experience.**

Read 1 John 3:16-18.

• **What does John want us to know about loving others?**

• **After reading this Scripture, how would you define the word *love*?**

• **What is one way you can show your love for someone this week, based on what you've just experienced?**

Topic: Materialism

Image Is Nothing

Scripture Focus: Matthew 6:19-21

Supplies: Bibles, 1 current magazine (fashion or sports magazines are best) for every 2 teenagers, paper, pens, newsprint, marker

The Activity

Ask students to look through magazines in pairs, making a tally mark on a piece of paper for every advertisement featuring a name brand type of clothing. Ask them to list the names as well. After five minutes, work with students to compile the lists on a piece of newsprint on the wall.

Discussion

• **Did looking at these ads make you want to buy these products?**

• **What was the main message the ads were trying to convey? How did they make you feel about yourself?**

• **Do you judge people by their clothes or the labels they wear? Do you feel people judge you based on materialistic things?**

• **Be honest—how much value do you place on your possessions?**

Read Matthew 6:19-21.

• **How can you apply the truth of this passage to your life?**

Topic: Mercy

Give Me Mercy

Scripture Focus: Ephesians 2:4-5

Supplies: Bibles, pens, paper

The Activity

Distribute a pen and piece of paper to each student. Take a pen and piece of paper for yourself, and ask the students to take a few minutes to write down every sin they can remember committing in the last month. Let them know that they won't be showing anyone else their lists, so they can be brutally honest. Then ask students to close their eyes and picture themselves in a court of law, listening to their sins read aloud and pleading guilty to each one.

> ### Always Be Prepared!
>
> This devotion may bring up some deep heart issues for students who've struggled with "serious" sins in their past, such as sexual sin, breaking the law, or repeated lying. Be prepared to talk in greater depth with students who need help understanding God's mercy in their lives.

Next, tell your students to write the punishment they think they deserve in large letters at the top of their lists.

Pick up your paper and rip it in half. Tell your students to do the same.

Say: **All of us sin, and the punishment we deserve is nothing less than death. But our God is rich in mercy. Instead of demanding the punishment we deserve, he meets our sins and failings with mercy, offering his own Son as payment for our sins.**

Discussion

• What is *mercy*?

• Is *mercy* justice? Why or why not?

• How does it feel to think about the mercy God has shown you?

Read Ephesians 2:4-5.

• How can we be assured of receiving God's mercy?

• How can we better show others the mercy God promises to us?

Topic: Missions

It's All Greek to Me

Scripture Focus: Isaiah 61:1

Supplies: Bibles; photocopies of the "Isaiah 61:1 Cards" handout (p. 18), cut apart to create 1 card for each pair

The Activity

Before this activity, photocopy the handout (p. 18), and cut apart the cards to create one card for each pair of students.

Begin by asking teenagers to form pairs. Give one person in each pair a card, and instruct students to try to explain to their partners what their cards say, but caution that they must explain the verse without using words. Give them about three minutes to convey the message in pantomime. Then ask the partners who were watching what the message was. After you've heard every version, ask someone to read aloud the verse on the card.

Discussion

• How did it feel to try to explain a complicated thought with only pantomime? How did it feel to try to interpret that message?

• Language can sometimes be an obstacle in missions. What are some other obstacles in missions?

• Do you know of any specific missionaries? Who are they? What do they do?

• How does the Scripture we read relate to missions?

• Mission work often proves most effective when missionaries demonstrate the gospel through actions as well as words. What are some creative ways you can show the gospel to others?

Topic: Obedience

Complete in Him

Scripture Focus: 1 John 2:5-6

Supplies: Bibles, bread, peanut butter, jelly, chocolate chips, knives, napkins

The Activity

Before the activity, set out all of the sandwich-making supplies.

Isaiah 61:1 Cards

"The Spirit of the Sovereign Lord is on me, because the Lord has anointed me to preach good news to the poor. He has sent me to bind up the brokenhearted, to proclaim freedom for the captives and release from darkness for the prisoners" (Isaiah 61:1).

"The Spirit of the Sovereign Lord is on me, because the Lord has anointed me to preach good news to the poor. He has sent me to bind up the brokenhearted, to proclaim freedom for the captives and release from darkness for the prisoners" (Isaiah 61:1).

Separate students into two groups, and ask a volunteer to lead each group in creating the "perfect" peanut butter and jelly sandwich. Explain that students in each group need to follow their leader's directions. The first volunteer should instruct his or her group in standard directions for making a peanut butter sandwich. The second volunteer should instruct his or her group to make a sandwich by spreading peanut butter and jelly on the *outside* of the sandwich, putting chocolate chips in the middle, on the plain sides of the bread, and cutting the sandwich into circles.

Allergies

Some people are seriously allergic to peanuts, so make sure you check with your students (or their parents) before doing this activity.

Invite teenagers to make and eat their sandwiches. Be sure the second group has lots of napkins!

Discussion

• Did your volunteer help you create the "perfect" peanut butter sandwich? Why or why not?

• What emotions and thoughts did you experience as you obeyed your leader's directions?

• How do you feel about obeying authority figures like parents or teachers? How do you feel about obeying God?

Read 1 John 2:5-6.

• What would it look like for someone to live out the meaning of this verse? Give examples.

• What is one step you can take to grow in your obedience to God?

Topic: Peace

Peace of the Rock

Scripture Focus: Romans 5:1-11

Supplies: Bibles, large piece of newsprint or poster board, markers

The Activity

Say: **A peace treaty is an agreement between two warring nations or two sides in a dispute. Both sides agree to seek peaceful solutions in spite of their differences. Often, it calls for each side to make concessions, or to offer something, or to compromise in some way for the sake of peace.**

Read Romans 5:1-11 aloud. Discuss the problem of sin and how it puts us at war with God. Ask your teenagers to help you create a peace treaty, using the Scripture passage as their starting point. Say: **In your treaty, make note of what God has offered in hope of a peaceful solution. The treaty should address things a Christian must do to accept the terms of God's offer and things he or she might need to give up or concede.**

Discussion
- **How does the world define *peace*? How does that differ from the peace God offers?**
- **Why does sin put us at odds with God?**
- **What is God's remedy for our sin problem? Explain.**
- **Why do some people find it difficult to accept God's offer?**
- **What are you willing to do or offer in light of God's peace offering?**

Topic: Peer Pressure

Molded

Scripture Focus: Proverbs 13:20

Supplies: Bibles, clay or modeling dough

The Activity

Set out several balls of clay or modeling dough, and allow teenagers to sit and create different works of art. Challenge them to pick partners and create their best renditions of those people. Explain that their creations do not have to be literal; instead of sculpting those people, they could create things that characterize their partners' interests or hobbies, such as a soccer ball or a guitar. When they've finished, allow the students to explain some of their creations and some of the difficulties they went through during their creative process.

Discussion
- **What was it like watching someone create a sculpture to represent you?**
- **Did the sculpture match who you really are? Why or why not?**
- **Was the experience of having a clay representation of yourself sculpted by another person similar to the way you are shaped by peer pressure? Explain.**

Read Proverbs 13:20.

• What does this verse tell us about the affects others can have on our lives? Do you agree with this verse? Why or why not?

• How can you apply the truth of this verse to your relationships with others?

Topic: Relationships

What's My Reputation?

Scripture Focus: John 13:34-35

Supplies: Bibles, small blank cards, pens

The Activity

Have teenagers sit in a circle, and give every student a couple of cards and a pen. Explain that on one card they should write down their answers to three general categories that you choose, such as hair color, brand of tennis shoes, and age. When they've finished, put all the cards in the center of the circle, and ask each teenager to draw one and guess who it belongs to. You'll probably find that there are several students who fit the description on the card. Now repeat the exercise with more unusual categories, such as favorite band, favorite vacation spot, and middle name. This second time it will be easier for students to discover the specific person.

Discussion

• In which round was it easier to identify the right person? Why?

• What are some other traits that distinguish you from others?

Read John 13:34-35.

• What did Jesus say would be the distinguishing feature of his disciples? Is this true of our group?

• In what ways can our love for each other be obvious to people around us?

• Does this mean you have to *like* everyone in the group? Explain.

• What can you do to make your relationships with others more Christlike?

Topic: Right Choices

One Way

Scripture Focus: Proverbs 12:15; 16:17

Supplies: Bibles, 2 sheets of newsprint (each at least 15 feet long), markers

The Activity

Roll out two long sheets of newsprint parallel to each other on the floor. Have students gather around the papers, and have volunteers

draw lines on each sheet to make them look like roads. Have another volunteer label one road as the "Way of the Righteous" and the other as the "Way of the Fool." Encourage students to discuss and draw landmarks and symbols that characterize each road. To get students thinking, mention some specific scenarios that require wise or foolish choices, such as, "You go to a party and people are drinking" or "You have a lot of homework, but your friend wants you to go to the mall." Encourage students to share specific choices that would lead someone down either of the roads. Prompt students to write words from the discussion on the appropriate road.

Discussion

Read Proverbs 12:15; 16:17.

• What is the difference between a fool and a wise person?

• Why is it foolish always to think your way is right?

• What does it mean to "guard your way"?

• When have you made choices that help you walk the way of righteousness? When have you made foolish choices? Share examples.

• What are some of the ways you can make choices that will help you stay on the right road?

Topic: Sharing One's Faith

See the Light

Scripture Focus: Luke 8:16

Supplies: Bibles, lots of flashlights (10 or more, depending on your group size)

The Activity

Before students arrive, position flashlights under tables and chairs in your room, and turn off the lights. Turn the flashlights on so that when the overhead lights are off, all the flashlights can be located by their light.

Give students one minute to locate as many flashlights as they can. When they find a flashlight, they should set it on top of something, such as a table or chair, so that the light is pointing up and is in plain view. (If you think one minute is too much time for your group, you could cut the time down to thirty seconds.)

> **Set The Mood!**
> *For added impact, you could leave the lights off with the flashlights still on during your discussion. Use one of the flashlights to read the Scripture.*

Discussion

Read Luke 8:16.

• **What do you think Jesus is referring to when he talks about not hiding your light?**

• **Why is it important to be open with others about our faith?**

• **Was it easier or harder to see the flashlights once they were set in plain view? Why?**

• **How is that like the way we live our lives as Christians?**

• **How can you show your light to someone this week?**

Topic: Sin

A Handful

Scripture Focus: Luke 18:18-25

Supplies: Bibles, at least 5 objects that represent sins a person might have in life (such as magazines to represent materialism, a telephone to represent busyness, a small TV to represent sloth), at least 5 other objects (such as a towel, a baseball, a CD, a pair of shoes, or a balloon), cup of water

The Activity

Pile all of the objects in the center of the room. Ask a volunteer to pick up and hold all of the objects in the pile.

Say: **We often sin when we try to satisfy ourselves with material things instead of with God. We can fill up our lives with sin until we can't hold anything else. And then Jesus comes along and promises to truly satisfy us...**

Set a cup of water on the floor in front of the volunteer. Ask the student to try to pick up the cup of water and drink it. Inevitably, either the objects or the cup will end up on the floor.

Say: **...and then you have to choose.**

Invite other eager students to try the same activity, picking up and holding all of the objects and then attempting to pick up and drink a cup of water.

Discussion

• **How was this experience like your life? How can your life get filled up with sin?**

Read Luke 18:18-25.

• **How did the ruler's life get filled up?**
• **When is it difficult to drop or let go of our sins or desires?**
• **How does Jesus satisfy us?**
• **What does Jesus offer us that our sins cannot?**

Topic: Trust

A Real Treat

Scripture Focus: Psalm 37:3-6

Supplies: Bibles, blindfolds, 1 chocolate candy for each student

The Activity

Have students split into pairs, and blindfold one person in each pair. Give a chocolate candy to the person in each pair who isn't blindfolded. Tell the blindfolded students that their partners are going to put something in their mouths. Don't give them any information about what it tastes like or whether it's even edible; just encourage them to trust their partners to give them something they're going to like. Have the teenagers with the candies put them in their partners' mouths. After that, have teenagers take off their blindfolds, and give "the feeders" a piece of candy too.

Discussion

• For those of you who were blindfolded, what did you think you were going to get?

• Was it difficult to trust your partner? Why or why not?

• How important is trust to a relationship? Explain.

Read Psalm 37:3-6.

• What will God do for you if you put your trust in him?

• How can having trust in God change your outlook on life?

Topic: Truth

Tripping Over Truth

Scripture Focus: John 10:1-5

Supplies: Bible, several paper or plastic-foam cups, blindfold

The Activity

Blindfold a volunteer, then take him or her out of the room. Invite students to help you clear an open playing area and then place several cups on the floor in various places throughout the room. The object is for the volunteer to find his or her way from one end of the room to the other without tripping over any cups. However, everyone else in the room is going to call out directions, some true and some false. Choose about one-third of the teenagers in the room whose job will be to provide truthful directions (avoiding the cups), and the other two-thirds will shout out false directions. Now bring the volunteer in, and let the directions begin.

After the volunteer has completed the task, say: **We live in a pluralistic world; there are a number of different voices and messages out there that will claim to be true. Some of those influences will steer you in the right direction, while many others will make you crash. It's important to know who you can trust.**

Discussion

- How do we know when something is true or trustworthy?

Read John 10:1–5.

- How do you "know" God's voice?
- How do you recognize the stranger's voice?
- What can happen in your life when you follow a misleading voice?
- What does your life look like when you listen to truth–to God's voice?

Event and Location Devotions

T ake a trip with these devotions that help you use a specific location or event to make a powerful biblical point. These devotions will help you turn a pool party or a visit to a bowling alley into a launchpad for discussion and life change. Each of these location and event suggestions includes questions that will kick-start an on-site five-minute discussion.

Topic: Bible Study

Map Masters

Scripture Focus: James 1:22-25

Location: Bus station or bus stop

Supplies: Bibles, 1 bus route map for each teenager

The Location Devotion

Take your teenagers to a local bus station. If there isn't one nearby, visit a local bus stop.

Before your meeting, get copies of the route map, and determine how to reach a specific spot on the route. When your group has gathered at the bus station, give teenagers a step-by-step briefing about how to make the trip to the location you've targeted—what bus to catch, when the bus arrives, what the fare will be, and so on. Distribute a route map to each teenager so that teenagers can follow along on the maps.

But when it's time to buy a ticket or step up onto the bus, announce that your students won't actually be going anywhere.

Say: **Hmmm...what we know about reaching a destination isn't worth much if we don't *act* on what we know. Just having information doesn't get us anywhere.**

Discussion

• What's something you know that you absolutely won't act on? (For example, you know that jumping off a tall building will hurt you, but you don't have to act on it to find out.)

Read James 1:22-25.

• What's something you know God wants you to do, but you don't often do it? Why?

• Is it easier to be a "listener" or "doer" of the Word? Why? Which word best describes you?

• Most Christians read the Bible at least occasionally. How do you feel when you do that? What are the benefits that Bible study brings to your life?

• How would you like to improve in your personal Bible study habits?

Topic: Celebration

Time to Party

Scripture Focus: Deuteronomy 14:22-26

Event: Pool party or swimming pool

Supplies: Bibles, swimsuits, towels

The Event Devotion

Plan a pool party for your teenagers. While they're swimming, see if you can get teenagers to dive for things you've tossed into the deep end, or challenge them to see how far they can swim underwater. Have a contest to see who can stay underwater the longest. Those who aren't confident swimmers can help time the people underwater.

When you're all back on dry land, gather students for a discussion.

Discussion

• How does it feel when you are gasping for breath? Why do we need to breathe oxygen?

Read Deuteronomy 14:22-26.

• What were the Israelites told to do with their tithe—one-tenth of everything their land had produced? Why?

• Spiritual disciplines are like oxygen to our faith, and celebration is one of the disciplines. What kind of celebration honors God?

• When and how did you last celebrate God's goodness and faithfulness?

• How can we celebrate God's goodness as a group?

Topic: Confession

Without One Plea

Scripture Focus: Psalm 38:18

Location: Courtroom

Supplies: Bibles, dictionary

The Location Devotion

Take your group to a courtroom. See if you can arrange to watch a trial in session or sit in an empty courtroom for your discussion. If you watch a live trial, encourage students to pay attention to how the defendant pleads. Afterward, discuss the trial or, if in an empty room, what happens in a trial.

Say: **In a trial, the defendant is invited to make a plea, guilty or not guilty. Defendants essentially can confess if they want to. If they plead guilty, they can often plea bargain, or receive a lesser sentence because they chose to confess.**

Get Legal Representation

Add impact to this devotion by inviting a lawyer or judge from your church or community to tag along and participate in the discussion.

Discussion

• Why do you think some defendants confess what they've done and plead guilty?

• Why do some people refuse to confess what they've done? How is that like everyday life?

Read Psalm 38:18.

• Why is confessing our sins to God important?

• What happens when you confess? How does it affect your life?

• Is confession of sin a regular part of your spiritual life? How do you want to grow in that area?

Topic: Creation

God's Signature

Scripture Focus: Romans 1:19-20

Location: Park

Supplies: Bibles, pens or pencils, index cards

The Location Devotion

Take teenagers to a park that has a large tree in it, and invite them to sit around the tree. Distribute index cards and pens or pencils, and invite students to observe the tree silently for a moment, recording their observations on their index cards. When they've finished, prompt students to share what they know about the process that causes a seed to grow into a large tree. Have a volunteer read aloud Romans 1:19-20, and allow teenagers another moment to write down their thoughts.

Discussion
- What types of observations did you write on your index cards?
- What does nature show you about God?
- Why is it hard for people to believe that God created the world?
- Romans 1:19-20 says that nature demonstrates God's existence and his design in the world. Do you see God's signature in the created world? Why or why not?
- What are some examples from nature that help you believe in God's power and divine nature?

Topic: Death

Beginnings and Endings

Scripture Focus: Hebrews 9:27-28

Location: Hospital maternity ward

Supplies: Bibles

The Location Devotion

Take your teenagers to a hospital maternity ward during visiting hours when you'll be allowed to see babies in the nursery.

Ask students to look at the babies and fix several of the babies' faces in their minds. Then lead your students outside the hospital to a place where they can see the windows of a patient wing.

Say: **The maternity floor is one place where nobody likes to talk about death, but it happens. Infants die every day. Parents who waited anxiously for nine months leave the hospital brokenhearted, feeling pain that may last a lifetime. They return home to face an empty crib in an empty nursery. And consider these windows; behind them are patients, some of whom will likely die here.**

> ### Call First!
> *Security at hospitals is usually very tight. Make sure you call ahead and make arrangements with the hospital for your tour of the maternity ward.*

Discussion

• If you were allowed to decide, how would you choose to die? While young or old? Quickly or slowly? Describe your idea of a "good death."

• Why is it so difficult to talk about death?

• We're all going to die. How do you feel about your death?

Read Hebrews 9:27-28.

• What do you think of the purpose for which Jesus gave his life? What does it mean to you?

• What's a cause that you'd willingly die for? Why?

Topic: Emotions

Take Me Out to the Ballgame

Scripture Focus: Romans 12:15

Event: Local or professional sporting event

Supplies: Bibles

The Event Devotion

Take your students to a local or professional sporting event, such as a high school soccer game or major league baseball game. Before the game, tell students to watch for the different emotions people express throughout the game—the referees, the players, the fans, the coaches. When the game is over, have teenagers share what they observed.

Discussion
• What events triggered emotions in the different people you observed?
• What events trigger emotions in your life?
Read Romans 12:15.
• When has a friend rejoiced or mourned with you? How did it feel?
• Why is it often valuable to have someone to share your emotions with?
• What are some ways that we can join others in their "mourning" or "rejoicing," even if we personally have nothing to do with their particular situations?

Topic: Friendship

By His Love

Scripture Focus: John 15:9-17

Location: Animal shelter (such as a local chapter of the Humane Society)

Supplies: Bibles

The Location Devotion

Take students to an animal shelter for a tour, and, if possible, interview the employees and volunteers. As you spend time with the animals and staff, encourage your students to ask questions about what the animals are being saved from and how they are cared for. After the tour, gather teenagers for discussion.

Discussion
• How are those animals being cared for? What might happen to them if this shelter weren't taking care of them?
• What are those people's motivations for what they do? Do you think they're being true friends to the animals? Explain.

Read John 15:9-17.

- **What does Jesus say about how and why we should love?**

- **What do you think these verses have to do with being a friend?**

- **How can you follow Jesus' words and the example of the people we met today in loving others?**

Topic: Gender

Ideals

Scripture Focus: Genesis 1:26-27

Event: Valentine's Day party

Supplies: Bibles, Valentine's Day party favors, snacks, paper, pens

The Event Devotion

Use the following discussion during a Valentine's Day party. After snacks or any party games you have planned, have all the girls get together and make a list of the top five characteristics of "the ideal guy," and have the guys create a similar list of "the ideal girl." Have the groups share their lists with each other.

Discussion

- **What are some of the stereotypes that exist about girls and guys? In other words, what is each "supposed" to be good at, what is each "supposed" to like, and so on?**

- **Do you generally find these stereotypes to be true about you and your friends? Why or why not?**

Read Genesis 1:26-27.

- **What does it mean that God created both men and women in his image?**

- **What does this tell us about God? Explain.**

- **What are some of the things that guys can learn from girls? What can girls learn from guys?**

Topic: God's Discipline

God's Gym

Scripture Focus: Proverbs 3:11-12

Location: Gym or fitness club

Supplies: Bibles

The Location Devotion

Take your group to a gym or fitness club. Arrange a tour if you can, and see if a few teenagers can try out some of the equipment. Ask one of the physical trainers to explain specifically how weight lifting makes muscles stronger.

Say: **Those of you who regularly work out know that lifting weights can make your muscles feel pretty sore. So why do you do it? Because stretching your muscles in that way is what makes them grow stronger.**

Discussion
• **What do you think of when you hear "God's discipline"?**

Read Proverbs 3:11-12.

• **Why would God discipline those he loves?**
• **What does it feel like to undergo God's discipline?**
• **How does it stretch you?**
• **How does it make you stronger?**

Topic: Jesus

The Word Became Flesh

Scripture Focus: John 1:14

Location: Carpenter's workshop or home construction site

Supplies: Bibles

The Location Devotion

Take your group to a carpenter's workshop, or visit a home construction site (with permission, of course!). Arrange to have a tour of the place, find out what projects

they're working on, and what kinds of things they've built in the past. After that, find a quiet spot to have a discussion.

Talk about how we hear a lot about Jesus' ministry, but one thing they may not know is that Jesus' human father, Joseph, was a carpenter, and Jesus learned his father's trade. Jesus is God's Son, the Savior of the world, but the fact that he was also a carpenter reminds us of his humanity as well. Jesus was human, just like us.

Discussion

Read John 1:14.

- Who is "the Word" in this passage?
- Why did God make his dwelling among us?
- What do you think Jesus' everyday life was like as a boy? a teenager? a man?
- What difference does it make to you that Jesus was human?
- How does Jesus' humanity help you relate to him?

Topic: Justice

Tenpin Justice

Scripture Focus: Ephesians 2:8-9

Event: Bowling

Supplies: Bibles

The Event Devotion

Go to a bowling alley, and spend some time bowling as a group. When you've finished, gather everyone for a discussion about justice.

Say: **Bowling is pure physics—absolute justice. The lane is flat; the balls are round; the pins are set up in precisely the same way every time, on every lane. Bowlers release their bowling balls and get exactly what they deserve. It's pure cause and effect, complete justice.**

Can you get lucky and throw a strike even when you're a beginner? Sure, but you only get a strike if you put the ball in the right place. It's a level playing field...always.

Strrrrrrrrrrrrike!

To really make your point, invite one of the bowling alley's resident "pros" to demonstrate a few strikes and spares for your group.

Discussion

• **How is life like a level playing field? unlike one? Explain.**

• **If you could snap your fingers and have everything in life be absolutely fair for everyone, including you, would you do it? Why or why not?**

• **Describe an injustice you've seen in the world this past week. What was it?**

Read Ephesians 2: 8-9.

• **If life were truly fair—one hundred percent just—what would that mean in your relationship with God? Explain.**

• **In what ways do you experience God's grace and give grace?**

Topic: Perseverance

Hang in There

Scripture Focus: Hebrews 10:36

Event: Trip to indoor climbing center

Supplies: Bibles

The Event Devotion

Take your students to an indoor climbing center where each student can experience climbing a wall and

holding the ropes for someone else as that person climbs. When you're ready to leave, take a few minutes in a quiet spot to have this devotion.

Say: **Hopefully you had a lot of fun climbing today, and perhaps you learned something about your strength. I don't mean physical strength; I mean the kind of mental strength you need to climb higher, even when you're scared.**

Next, talk about how climbing the walls is similar to the way we live our lives. Sometimes we are challenged to do things that we might be scared to do or may not feel we have the strength to do. The same is true for our Christian walk. But when we face those situations, God wants us to keep going so that we can become stronger.

Discussion

• **How did you feel about climbing the wall? Was it easy or difficult?**

• **How did you feel about being a support for someone else as he or she climbed?**

Read Hebrews 10:36.

• **What does this verse have to do with our climbing experience?**

• **How is persevering like trying to "climb" in your Christian faith?**

• How can you be a support for someone else as he or she perseveres in life?

Topic: Poverty

Life on a Dollar a Day

Scripture Focus: Amos 5:11-14

Location: Grocery store

Supplies: Bibles, 1 dollar for each student

The Location Devotion

Take your group to a grocery store, and give each student one dollar. Tell students to imagine that they must buy a healthy dinner for themselves using nothing more than the dollar. Also, tell them that they may not team up and pool their resources—they can only buy one dollar's worth of food.

When everyone has finished, ask students to show each other what they bought. Then say: **Many of the poor in industrialized countries are not actually homeless or jobless. They have a source of income, and sometimes two jobs, but can't make enough money to pay all of the bills.**

Donate the Goods

After the discussion, invite the students to donate all the food they bought to a ministry for the needy or to your church's food pantry.

Discussion

• What does it feel like to have too little to get by on?

Read Amos 5:11-14.

• How does God respond if we ignore the poor?

• Why do you think some people are poor?

• How does your lifestyle affect the welfare of others?

• How does God want us to respond to poverty? Give examples.

Topic: Pride

Standing Proud?

Scripture Focus: Proverbs 16:5

Location: Flagpole

Supplies: Bibles

The Location Devotion

Take your students to the nearest flagpole, such as at one of the schools nearby. Call an official beforehand to ask if your youth group can fulfill the task of lowering the flag at the end of the day. After you have folded it properly and put it away, ask your students what the flag means to them.

Discussion

• **Are you proud of being a citizen of this country? If so, what form does your pride take? What does it mean to you?**

Read Proverbs 16:5.

• **What kind of pride does God warn us against?**

• **Is some pride OK, such as pride in school or country or religion? Why or why not?**

• **What do you take the most pride in? What would God think of your pride?**

• **How can you use your pride in God's service?**

Topic: The Resurrection

A Fellow Traveler?

Scripture Focus: Luke 24:13–35

Location: Country road, dirt path, or path in a park

Supplies: Bibles

The Location Devotion

Drive to a spot outside of town, and take your group for an enjoyable walk down a deserted country road or park pathway. While you're walking, slowly read Luke 24:13–35 aloud.

Discussion

• Jesus' very first resurrection appearances were to unlikely people—some women and two people hardly mentioned in Scripture. Why do you think he chose to appear to them first instead of to the disciples or religious leaders?

• Why do you think many of the people Jesus appeared to after his death had a hard time recognizing him?

• What do you think Jesus might have explained to the travelers about the Scriptures and about himself while walking on the road?

• The two travelers immediately headed back for Jerusalem after seeing Jesus; they didn't even wait until dawn. How can you develop this kind of passion and excitement about the resurrection of Christ?

• How does Christ's resurrection impact your own life?

Topic: Salvation

Never in Short Supply

Scripture Focus: John 4:10-14

Location: Waterfall, lake, river, stream, or water fountain

Supplies: Bibles

The Location Devotion

Take your group hiking to a place where you will have access to a waterfall or other body of water, such as a lake, river, stream, or water fountain. After you've done some hiking, stop at the waterfall or body of water, and lead this devotion. If it's possible for your group to do so, have them sit along the edge of the water.

Say: **We hear a lot about conservation of our energy, water, plants, and land, among other things. It opens our eyes to the fact that we may not have an infinite supply of those things and reminds us that we should be careful not to waste what we have. But there is something that Jesus tells us we have access to that will never run out.**

Encourage students to put either a hand or foot in the water (if the weather isn't too cold) as you read aloud John 4:10-14.

Discussion
- What is Jesus referring to in the Scripture passage when he talks about "living water"?
- Why does he call salvation living water?
- What does Jesus teach us about salvation in the Scripture passage?
- How can knowing you have access to "living water" change the way you live your life?

Topic: Stewardship

Ringin' in the Money

Scripture Focus: Matthew 10:8b

Event: Service project, such as Salvation Army bell ringers

Supplies: Bibles

The Event Devotion

Have your students volunteer as Salvation Army bell ringers (or as collectors for another cause you choose together). If your group is small enough to take one shift, work with them and take them out for hot chocolate afterward to talk about the experience. If you have a large group, organize them to work during the same time at different locations, and ask everyone to gather afterward at the church for a discussion.

Discussion
- What did you observe today?
- Were the people you expected to be generous the ones who gave money?
- The management and giving of one's money and other resources is generally known as *stewardship*. Did asking for donations affect how you feel about stewardship? Why or why not?

Read Matthew 10:8b.
- Why does God ask us to "freely give"?
- Do you give freely of your money? or of your other resources, such as time and friendship? What resource can you give more of?

Topic: Temptation

Our Daily Bread

Scripture Focus: Matthew 6:8-13

Location: Fast-food restaurant

Supplies: Bibles, playing cards or board games

The Location Devotion

Before the devotion, arrange with a fast-food restaurant to allow your group to sit for up to thirty minutes before ordering. Also verify that no one in your group will be at a health risk if they have to wait for a while before eating.

Invite your group to lunch or dinner, making sure you select a time to eat when everyone will be hungry. When you arrive at the restaurant, have everyone take a seat rather than order. Challenge your group members to see how long they can wait before ordering their meals. While teenagers are waiting, you may want to keep them occupied with games.

After about thirty minutes, suggest to teenagers that they can order when they are ready.

Say: **It wasn't easy to resist eating when we're surrounded by the sights, smells, and sounds of good food cooking. This is a lot like other temptations we face—they surround us every day.**

Discussion
- **How hard was it to resist eating?**
- **What are some other temptations you face that are hard to resist?**
- **What are some simple ways to resist those temptations?**

Read Matthew 6:8-13.

- **How can prayer help you resist temptation?**
- **What is one area in your life in which you need God's help to resist temptation?**

Topic: Tragedy

Always There

Scripture Focus: Romans 8:28-39

Location: Cemetery

Supplies: Bibles

The Location Devotion

Take your students to visit a cemetery. Give them some time to wander around and look at the gravestones.

Call them back together, and ask them to sum up how they feel in one or two words. Then send them back to look at the gravestones again, specifically looking at the statements that say how much people were loved. Ask them to imagine the good things these people did, the things they created, the people they helped. Remind them that a cemetery may seem at first to be a very gloomy place, but it can actually be seen as a celebration of lives gone by.

Discussion

• What statements did you find that showed how much people have been loved? How do you think these people are remembered by those who love them?

• Death is obviously a tragic event. What other tragedies do people have to face in life?

Read Romans 8:28-39.

• What is God's promise to us when we're in the midst of tragedy?

• What tragedies or circumstances have made you feel separated from God? How do these verses make you feel?

• Sometimes when something awful happens, people may *know* these verses are true, but still *feel* like God is far away. How can you support and encourage people during those times?

Topic: Wisdom

Older and Wiser

Make an Appointment

Before you go to the retirement home, call ahead and ask the activity director when would be a good time to visit. Also, find out which halls house the more healthy patients who would be better able to interact with your teenagers.

Scripture Focus: Job 28:28

Location: Retirement home

Supplies: Bibles

The Location Devotion

Take your teenagers to a local retirement home. Instruct students to form pairs and spend time meeting and talking to residents. While visiting with the residents, teenagers should tell them that they are studying wisdom and ask the residents what wisdom means to them.

At a set time, have the group get back together, and ask them to share the various responses they heard.

Discussion

• We often think wisdom is a characteristic of the elderly. Did you find that to be true today?

• Did what you heard change your ideas of what wisdom is?

Read Job 28:28.

• Is this how you normally define wisdom?

• Where does wisdom come from?

• Are you making wise choices in your life?

Need a unique real-life story or a funny fictional tale to illustrate a Bible truth? Here you'll find short, five-minute or less, startling, funny, inspiring, and compelling illustrations that will get your teenagers thinking more deeply about important spiritual topics. Simply read the illustration aloud to your group, then use the discussion questions to help students understand how to apply biblical principles to their lives.

Topic: Alcohol and Drugs

99 Bottles of Beer on the Wall

Scripture Focus: Ephesians 5:17-18

Supplies: Bibles

The Illustration

Amy Carr, nineteen, is a top student—a *very* top student.

The Lancashire, England, teenager bested 370,000 A-level entrants to win an academic prize awarded in London.

As a student at Lancaster Girls' Grammar School, Carr gained A-level grades in German, French, English Literature, and General Studies. Her excellent academic record not only earned her a silver medal in languages, but also a gold medal and a check for approximately $360 as one of ten top finalists overall.

When reached for comment by BBC News, Carr said that to celebrate, she'll probably spend her prize money on German beer.

Discussion

• Why do you think alcohol is so often associated with celebrations?

• Nothing in Carr's academic career or the news reports about her indicates she's addicted to alcohol, but what do you think of her comment about spending her prize money to buy alcohol?

- What's your view of alcohol use? Why?

Read Ephesians 5:17-18.

- How do you think God views alcohol? Why?

- How do you need to apply biblical principles about alcohol to your own life?

Topic: Cheating

Honest Gain

Scripture Focus: Ezekiel 18:7-9

Supplies: Bibles

The Illustration

Thief Randy Griffin found an ingenious way to steal diamonds. He switched two real diamonds with fake ones and then swallowed the real ones in order to steal them more easily.

When the police caught up with him and he was X-rayed, one diamond showed up—inside Griffin. Apparently, after initially denying the theft, he admitted what he had done because he was afraid of internal injuries. For days after the incident, both the thief and authorities waited expectantly for him to pass the stolen diamonds.

Discussion

- What motivated Griffin to do what he did?

- How would you define the word *cheat*? In what ways did Randy try to cheat?

• What are some examples of common types of cheating? What are some consequences of cheating?

Read Ezekiel 18:7-9.

• What does this Scripture say about what happens to someone who lives in honesty and doesn't cheat? How does this apply to real life?

• How do you think God helps us lead lives of truth and honesty?

Topic: Compassion

Looking After Those He Loves

Scripture Focus: James 1:27

Supplies: Bibles

The Illustration

A group of people traveled to China for sightseeing and to visit an orphanage there. Three women in the group were deeply moved by the health condition of an infant boy they saw there. He was in dire need of surgery; without it he would die in a matter of days.

Instead of continuing on with their tour, the women immediately took the orphan boy to the hospital. When the doctor asked why they wanted to help this child that they didn't even know, they responded by saying, "We are Christians and it is our duty to help him."

The doctor readied his staff immediately and worked overtime to perform the surgery that day. Miraculously, the little boy's life was saved, and the effort only cost the women about $250.

(This story is adapted with permission from "In His Grip" (Summer 2001), a publication of A Helping Hand Adoption Agency.)

Discussion

• Realistically, do you think many people would respond like the women in this situation did? How do you respond to situations of need?

Read James 1:27.

• What does God ask us to do in this verse? Why do you think he specifically mentions widows and orphans?

• How would you define *compassion* in your own words?

• Has anyone ever treated you with compassion? What was that experience like?

• How do you think God might be leading you to show compassion for someone?

Topic: Courage

A Streak of Courage

Scripture Focus: Deuteronomy 31:6

Supplies: Bibles

The Illustration

An eighteen-year-old young man recently entertained the lunchtime crowd at the Dutchman Essenhaus restaurant in Middlebury, Indiana, when he ran through the restaurant waving a flag and wearing *only* a fake beard and green hat. Lunchtime patrons were surprised, to say the least. "I think people were amused by it more than anything," said Middlebury Police Department Sergeant Kevin Miller in *The Truth of Elkhart*. The police are still searching for the suspect.

Discussion

• Have you ever performed or seen someone perform a prank like this one?

• Do you think the young man demonstrated courage? Why or why not?

Read Deuteronomy 31:6.

• What makes an action courageous? What makes a person courageous?

• What kind of courage does God ask of us?

• In what area of your life do you need to ask God for courage?

Topic: Dating

Pucker Up

Scripture Focus: Philippians 1:9-10

Supplies: Bibles

The Illustration

When Katie Rehn and Tim McAfee kissed at their wedding in Bismarck, North Dakota, it was a kiss to remember. It was the first time they had kissed. Ever.

During their two years of dating, the couple decided to live by a biblical standard of purity...and then some. They decided to not kiss until standing at the altar during their wedding.

Katie's parents supported the idea and usually prayed with the couple before Katie and Tim left the house on dates.

Because the couple focused on talking about important issues and getting to know each other rather than kissing and other sexual conduct, Katie's mother says Katie and Tim are likely far ahead of some couples who have been married for years.

Discussion

• Do you admire Tim and Katie, pity them, or feel something in between? Explain.

• Dating without any intimate physical contact, even kissing, is a rarity. Do you think it's a good idea? Why or why not?

• If someone asked you to date and suggested keeping this level of sexual purity, how would you respond? Why?

Read Philippians 1:9-10.

• In what ways can you live this out in your own dating relationships?

• What seems most challenging about doing so?

Topic: Endurance

A Leg to Stand On

Scripture Focus: 2 Timothy 4:7-8

Supplies: Bibles

The Illustration

It was a hot day in 1992 when a starter pistol sent Derek Redmond, one of Great Britain's track stars, sprinting down the racetrack at the Summer Olympics in Barcelona. Years of training had brought him to a point where just a few seconds would decide his true greatness. The crowds roared, his heart pounded, and his legs moved like pistons. But suddenly, all of his training came to a crashing end as his hamstring muscle snapped within his leg. He fell to the ground, defeated. The other runners raced ahead, leaving him slumped on the track, his hopes and dreams destroyed.

Suddenly, a man came running from the stands to Derek's side. Rather than a crazed fan, it turned out to be Derek's father. His father scooped him up in his arms, whispered encouragement in his ear, and began to walk with his son. They did not walk off the course. They began to walk toward the finish line, arm in arm, father and son. Derek was racked with pain from his leg. Still his father helped him on. Derek would not win. He would not take a medal. But he would finish the race that he set out to run. He would endure to the end. And he could do it because he was cradled in the arms of his father.

Discussion

• How do you think it felt for Derek Redmond when he crossed the finish line? What helped him endure?

Read 2 Timothy 4:7-8.

• What finish line is Paul talking about here? What does he mean by "fight" and "race"?

• How do you endure to the finish line of life?

• What might cause you to fall?

• How does God help you endure until you cross the line?

Topic: God the Father

What to Buy the God Who Has Everything

Scripture Focus: Psalm 68:4-5

Supplies: Bibles

The Illustration

Tara was a young girl who wanted to buy her dad a Father's Day present. Her mother told her to choose whatever she wanted, but Tara couldn't think of anything, so she decided to ask for help.

First, Tara asked a friend what to buy. Her friend had grown up with a single mother and was not in the habit of buying Father's Day presents, so he suggested, "I usually buy perfume and flowers on Mother's Day. Why don't you try that?"

Deciding this was not a good idea, Tara asked another friend. The second friend said that her mom was taking her father on a boat cruise and suggested Tara do the same. Tara thought this was a good idea, but then remembered that her dad didn't know how to swim and was deathly afraid of the water. It was a good Father's Day gift, but not for her father.

Eventually, she decided to ask her older brother what to get Dad for Father's Day. Her brother said that he had asked their dad what he wanted and that Dad had said he wanted a power drill. Finally, Tara knew just what she wanted to buy.

Like Tara, Christians seek to know and please God. Those who don't know God or who believe in another religion and worship another god can't know the Father like Christians can. Christians have a special relationship with God—the relationship of a father and his children.

> **Discussion**
> • Why were Tara's friends unable to help her decide on a gift? How is this similar to how our relationships with God differ from those who have different beliefs about God?
> • How is God like and unlike our human fathers?
> Read Psalm 68:4-5.
> • How is God a father to the fatherless?
> • How might someone who doesn't believe in God fail to understand

what God wants from us? What if someone believes in a god but is not a Christian?

• What do we gain from knowing God as our heavenly Father?

Topic: Hatred

The Ugliest Side

Scripture Focus: Galatians 5:19-21

Supplies: Bibles

The Illustration

According to the United States' Bureau of Justice Statistics, 60 percent of hate crimes are violent crimes, such as threats of bodily harm and assault. The remaining 40 percent of hate crimes involve property offences, such as property damage, destruction, or vandalism. Hate crimes are motivated by hatred of someone because of his or her race, ethnicity, sexual orientation, disability, or religion. Government statistics indicate that *teenagers* are to blame for the majority of hate crimes.

Discussion

• How would you define a hate crime? What do you think motivates people to commit hate crimes?

• Why do you think teenagers are responsible for the most hate crimes? How do you respond to that fact?

• Would you describe your age group as "hateful"? Why or why not?
Read Galatians 5:19-21.

• This Scripture describes hatred as part of our sinful nature. Why is hatred such a common problem? How do you struggle with it?

• What are some things that teenagers can do to help stop the tendency some young people have to turn their emotions into hate?

Topic: Honesty

When Good Things Happen to Bad People

Scripture: Proverbs 24:26

Supplies: Bibles

The Illustration

Victor Hugo's famous novel *Les Miserables* tells the fictional story of Jean Valjean, an ex-convict living in France in the nineteenth century.

As a young man living in poverty, Jean couldn't stand to watch his family starve, so he broke into a bakery and stole a loaf of bread. He was imprisoned for this for nineteen years and became a very bitter man.

When Jean was finally released on parole, a kind priest showed him compassion and took him in. But Jean's bitterness and instinct to survive got the best of him, and one night he stole the priest's expensive silver and took off. He was soon caught by the police, but when he was brought back to the priest, something wonderful happened. The priest not only welcomed Jean back, but he gave Jean *all the rest* of his silver, which was worth a small fortune! With this deed, the priest said to Jean, "You have promised me to become an honest man. I am purchasing your soul."

The priest's forgiveness and blessing changed Jean's life forever. His bitterness and dishonesty were transformed into kindness, honesty, and generosity.

Discussion

• Was the priest stupid to invite a dishonest thief into his home? He *did* pay the price for it: His silver was stolen. Defend your answer.

• The priest's grace and forgiveness motivated Jean's new commitment to honesty. How can Jesus' grace and forgiveness motivate us to live honestly?

Read Proverbs 24:26.

• Why is honesty compared to a kiss? What else can you compare it to?

• When is honesty difficult to live out? Give examples.

• How can you be strengthened to live honestly?

Topic: Hypocrisy

As Plastic as Barbie

Scripture Focus: Matthew 23:23-28

Supplies: Bibles

The Illustration

Ten years ago, Cindy Jackson decided she needed a new look: the Barbie look. Seriously, she wanted to look just like Barbie.

She has since spent about $85,000 on face-lifts, nose jobs, chin reductions, and liposuction and now says, "I'm just as plastic as [Barbie] is. And it's wonderful."

Her enthusiasm for cosmetic surgery has not stopped there. A thirty-three-year-old man from Britain contacted her, saying that he wanted to follow her example. They have chosen the perfect features for him from different celebrities: Brad Pitt's nose, Tom Cruise's cheekbones, and Keanu Reeves' lips. After about $50,000 worth of surgery, he has become her very own Ken doll.

Discussion

• What can cosmetic surgery change about a person? What can't it change?

Read Matthew 23:23-28.

• Do you see any similarities between the Pharisees and "Barbie" and "Ken"? What are they?

• Jesus calls the Pharisees hypocrites because their hearts were so different from their public image. What were they like on the inside?

• How righteous and holy do you look from the outside? What is your inside like?

• Jesus told the Pharisees to sort out their hearts first. What do you need to do to get your heart right with God?

Topic: Integrity

One-Day Millionaires

Scripture Focus: Proverbs 11:3

Supplies: Bibles

The Illustration

Imagine going to an ATM to get cash for a date and noticing something unusual: an extra $924 million in your checking account.

This actually happened to over eight hundred people in Chicago one Friday in 1996. Apparently First National Bank of Chicago accidentally credited over $700 *billion* total to the accounts of some of its customers. It was the greatest banking error in U.S. history. Amazing!

Even more amazing is this fact: No one ran off with the money.

Discussion

• If you were in that situation, would you have been tempted to take the $924 million? What would you have done with it?

• Are you surprised that no one took the money? Why or why not?

• What does *integrity* mean? What are the characteristics of someone with integrity?

Read Proverbs 11:3.

• How does integrity guide and duplicity destroy?

• How can you develop integrity?

Topic: Patience

Waiting for God

Scripture Focus: Colossians 1:9-14

Supplies: Bibles

The Illustration

Salomon Vides is learning about life with mobile phones, fast food, and computers after having spent thirty-two years in the Guatemalan jungle, hiding from a war that wasn't happening. In 1969 El Salvador invaded Honduras, and Vides escaped into the jungle for safety. Unknown to him, the war lasted for only four days. He fled deep into the forest, away from all signs of civilization, eating palm roots and turtles and wearing

a tunic made of monkey skin.

Rumors about sightings of a wild jungle man began to spread, and his brothers went to see if it was Salomon. Once they found him, they brought him home as a national celebrity. Vides now looks back on his years in the jungle as a very happy time in his life.

Discussion

• What was Vides waiting for? Did he have any way of knowing whether it had happened?

• Is Vides a good example of patience? Why or why not?

Read Colossians 1:9-14.

• Why do Christians need patience and endurance? What are we waiting for?

• How good are you at waiting for things?

• How does your waiting and patience need to be different from Vides'?

Topic: Persecution

A Very Real Battle

Scripture Focus: John 17:14-18

Supplies: Bibles

The Illustration

Heather Mercer and Dayna Curry were working for a Christian humanitarian organization in Afghanistan when they were jailed by the Taliban on August 3, 2001. They were arrested for trying to convert Muslims to Christianity, a crime considered punishable by death under the Taliban's rule. At the time, it was also illegal for an Afghan to convert to Christianity, and the penalty for doing so was death.

As Mercer and Curry awaited trial, their future became very scary and uncertain. They were imprisoned for three months, surviving bomb attacks, being held hostage in numerous prisons, sitting through long interrogations, and experiencing other difficulties. They knew that they would probably be put to death for their actions.

Amazingly they were freed by the Taliban and rescued by the military. They were then taken to Pakistan, where they reunited with their families and then headed home to America.

Discussion

• How were Curry and Mercer persecuted? How were Afghan converts to Christianity persecuted?

• What are the dangers of being a Christian? Is it dangerous to be a Christian in this country? in other countries?

Read John 17:14-18.

• How did Jesus pray for Christians who would be persecuted?

• In his prayer, Jesus said the world hated his disciples. Is this true? How have you experienced this? How do others experience this?

• Where can you find strength when you're faced with persecution?

On Bended... Dinner Tray?

Scripture Focus: Luke 5:16

Supplies: Bibles

The Illustration

Since the 1950s, the cadets at the Virginia Military Institute have followed the same routine. Every night before dinner, the cadets file into the dining hall, and one of them reads an ecumenical prayer before they sit and eat.

But two cadets, Neil Melon and Paul Knick, have challenged the long-standing tradition, arguing that publicly led prayer is neither appropriate nor legal in a state-funded university like VMI. The American Civil Liberties Union has brought suit against the school on behalf of the two cadets, who complain that the prayer promotes religion and makes non-participants feel excluded. The school's attorney, Solicitor General William Hurd, argues that the prayer is constitutional because no one is required to pray.

Discussion

• Do you pray in public? over meals? What are your feelings about public prayer?

• Do you ever ask non-Christians to join you in prayer, such as before a meal? Why or why not?

• What are the differences between the way you pray in public and how you pray in private? Do you consider one better than the other? Explain.

Read Luke 5:16.

• Although Jesus led his disciples in prayer, he also often prayed alone. At what times do you find yourself wanting to withdraw and pray?

• How can you strengthen your private prayer life? your public prayer life?

Topic: Satan

Officially Uninvited

Scripture Focus: 1 Peter 5:8-9

Supplies: Bibles

The Illustration

Satan is *officially* not welcome in the small town of Inglis, Florida.

At the four entrances to the town, hollowed-out signposts painted with the words *Repent, Request*, and *Resist* each contain an official proclamation written on city stationery and stamped with a gold seal. The proclamation, penned by the mayor of Inglis, Carolyn Risher, declares, "Be it known from this day forward that Satan, ruler of darkness, giver of evil, destroyer of what is good and just, is not now, nor ever again will be, a part of this town of Inglis...

"As blood-bought children of God, we exercise our authority over the devil in Jesus' name. By that authority, and through His Blessed Name, we command all satanic and demonic forces to cease their activities and depart the town of Inglis...

"Signed and sealed this 5th Day of November, 2001."

Discussion

• Do you think this proclamation will actually keep Satan out of Inglis, Florida? Why or why not?

• How does popular culture (movies, songs, TV shows, stories, and so on) depict Satan? Are these depictions correct? Explain.

• What is your personal understanding of who Satan is and what Satan is like? What does Satan have the power to do?

Read 1 Peter 5:8-9.

• How does this Scripture make you feel? Frightened? Empowered? Why?

• How can you resist Satan's efforts to discourage your spiritual growth.

Topic: School

Higher Education

Scripture Focus: Daniel 1:3-5, 17-20

Supplies: Bibles

The Illustration

You may have never thought of it before, but schools were actually invented at one point, and they were created with a purpose: Education was viewed as an important part of Christian faith.

The first English-speaking university, Oxford, began around 1096. From the very beginning, it was known as a center for theological study and religious discussion. Harvard University, the oldest college in the United States, was founded by Christian Pilgrims and focused primarily on general academics, as well as Puritan philosophy. Princeton, another of America's earliest universities, was founded by Presbyterians who wanted to prepare graduates to be well equipped for both civil service and church leadership.

Higher education is an important part of Christian history. Schools helped students understand the Bible and study the world that God created. Math and science investigated God in nature. Literature and languages showed how to communicate the gospel. School was invented to serve God.

Discussion
• What is your general attitude about school? Do you like it or dislike it? Why?

• Do you see education as an essential part of your faith? Why or why not? Read Daniel 1:3-5, 17-20.

• How were studies God's gift to Daniel and his friends?

• How would it change your studies if you believed you were doing them for God?

• How can you use your education to serve God? Be specific.

Topic: Self-Control

None for Me, Thanks

Scripture Focus: Galatians 5:22-23

Supplies: Bibles

The Illustration

During Ramadan, the daily lives of Muslims are turned upside down. For about a month, almost all Muslims over nine years old abstain from drink, food, tobacco, and sex during the day. Some are so strict that they won't even swallow their own saliva. Because of the strict rules about eating, many sleep during the day and work and play at night.

In countries where most people are Muslim, the day actually begins when the sun goes down, with a large meal called an *iftar*. Family visits, social interactions, and even business transactions take place during the middle of the night. Between 3:00 and 5:00 a.m. is another meal, then prayers, and, finally, bed.

Discussion

• It takes a lot of self-control to refrain from eating and drinking during each day for a month. Do you consider the strict rules of Ramadan to be extreme or to be a positive example of spiritual discipline? Explain.

• Do you practice any Christian disciplines, such as fasting, planned prayer, or Bible study time? What are the benefits of practicing these disciplines?

• How are spiritual disciplines related to self-control?

Read Galatians 5:22-23.

• Why is self-control one of the fruits of the Spirit? Why does God ask us to be self-controlled?

• Which areas of your life particularly require self-control?

Topic: Self-Image

Real Beauty

Scripture Focus: Psalm 139

Supplies: Bibles

The Illustration

You may not know her name, but you probably know her face. Laura Krauss Calenberg has modeled for Cosmopolitan magazine and companies such as Christian Dior and Neiman Marcus.

Laura began her modeling career when she was nineteen years old, and she quickly became rich and successful. But as her career was on the rise, her personality was on the decline. Laura describes this time in her life, saying, "I became an egotistical, self-centered person living a very self-centered life...'Me,' 'myself,' and 'I' were my three favorite words. My entire life was focused on my weight and my hair and my clothing and my overall appearance and attractiveness."

In an effort to keep climbing the career ladder, Laura began working non-stop, seven days a week, until her health made her slow down. Her overwork caused her to become sick, and one day she fainted during a photo shoot and injured her knee. Suddenly she was forced to slow down, and she had time to think.

Laura began to realize how empty her life had become; though she was beautiful and successful on the outside, she was missing meaning and significance on the inside. Her life felt shallow and empty.

During her illness, Laura reconnected with the Christian faith she'd had as a young teenager.

As she refocused on her relationship with God, she found her true value. Laura believes that a relationship with God "enables you to be free to accept and love yourself" for the right reasons.

Laura Krauss Calenberg is still a successful model, but her faith in Christ now takes center stage in her life.

Discussion

- Why do you think Laura became so self-centered?
- How did her self-image affect her actions? How does your self-image affect your actions?
- Is self-image a problem in our culture? Explain.

Read Psalm 139.

- Compare the message of this psalm with the messages of our culture. How is God's view of self-image countercultural?
- How do you need to adjust your own self-image to better reflect God's view of you?

Topic: Servanthood

Catch of the Day

Scripture Focus: 1 Peter 4:10-11

Supplies: Bibles

The Illustration

In Oslo, Norway, a fisherman hooked a big one: a 247-pound Danish angler named Kjell Ovesen, who had fallen into the Gaula river! Ovesen nearly drowned before Wilhelmsen saw him floating by. A quick cast snagged the sixty-year-old Dane, and Wilhelmsen reeled him in. Wilhelmsen's quick thinking (and strong fishing pole) saved Ovesens' life.

Discussion

• Wilhelmsen saved Ovesen's life. What do you think would be an appropriate reward for this action? Why?

• Describe a time you helped another person or another person helped you. What happened?

Read 1 Peter 4:10-11.

• Wilhelmsen had a good cast to use in serving others, especially Ovesen. What gift do you have that could be used to serve others?

• In what ways are you using it to serve others?

• What gifts are others using to serve and encourage you?

Topic: Sexual Abstinence

Trash or Treasure?

Scripture Focus: Song of Songs 7:10-12; 8:4

Supplies: Bibles

The Illustration

There once was a hermit who lived in a shabby cottage on the edge of town. He had no friends and no family. He had a beard down to his bellybutton and smelled like an armpit all over. The old, crusty hermit didn't have many possessions to be proud of, and when he died, everything he owned was carted away to a landfill.

But one item, a small monkey lamp, tumbled off the back of the dump truck and onto the street. The paint was scuffed in the fall, and the shade was crumpled a little. The monkey lamp had been a favorite of the hermit and, sadly, was now considered roadside garbage.

Some boys on bikes came upon the strange object lying in the street.

"Aw, it's just a stupid lamp," said one boy, kicking it onto the curb.

"Why don't people ever throw out cool stuff, like DVDs?" asked his friend. The two hopped back on their bikes, whizzing out of sight.

A jogger stopped for a moment to study the lamp lying on the curb. "Good grief, I live in a town of slobs," she said, spitting her gum into the grass.

Many people shuffled by the lamp, kicking it aside or trampling it underfoot. Finally, a young girl scooped it up and ran home to show her parents. Her mother wasn't at all impressed with the homely lamp.

"That's filthy!" she said and insisted her daughter now take a bath, which of course her daughter hated. The lamp was then tossed inside a box of items headed for a charity in town. The box was dropped off later that day.

"I'm sorry," the volunteer said with a smile, "but we are chock-full of funny-looking lamps." She motioned to a whole row of absurd-looking lamps that featured everything from Elvis to the California Raisins.

"I'll take it," said a passerby. "I'm having a garage sale tomorrow."

The lamp was placed on a crowded table early the next morning, along with dozens of empty pickle jars and a baby doll that's right eye had been blacked out with a Sharpie marker.

The sale had gone on for hours. All of the pickle jars were sold. Even the pirate-eyed doll now had a home. At last someone was taking a good, long look at the monkey lamp.

"I'll give you a nickel," she said to the owner.

"For the lamp?" asked the owner.

"No, for the light bulb," the lady said, unscrewing it from the socket.

An observer quickly approached the two women.

"May I look at that lamp?" he said, curiously.

The lady handed him the lamp for inspection, clutching onto the bulb.

"I'll pay you $3000 for this lamp!" the man exclaimed. Excitement overtook him, and he did a little dance move right there in the yard.

After the owner was revived with smelling salts, she agreed to the sale. She began dreaming of all the shoes she could buy.

"Is the lamp really that valuable?" she asked the man.

"Why this lamp is worth at least five times that amount!" he replied. "This is the finest monkey lamp I have ever seen!" With that said, he pulled on the tail of the monkey lamp. To the woman's amazement, the monkey's mouth dropped open, revealing a brilliant emerald the size of a golf ball!

The man carried the lamp home with two hands, like he was holding a baby. The priceless lamp was placed in an airtight glass case, safe from the harmful effects of artificial lighting and humidity. The valuable and one-of-a-kind monkey luminary became a popular attraction on bus tours, even more popular than the famed "World's Largest Ball of Yarn"! People traveled from near and far to catch a glimpse of the treasure that was once mistaken as trash.

Discussion

• **What are some things that are often undervalued?**

• **In what ways can people sell themselves too cheaply?**

Read Song of Songs 7:10-12; 8:4.

• **What worth does God place on your sexuality?**

• **What do teenagers sometimes exchange sex for? How can you value your body the way God intended you to?**

• **Why is it important to have sex only with your husband or wife?**

The Scoop on
Movie and Music Devotions

ere you'll find ideas for using pop culture to communicate God's truth. These short movie-clip and popular-song suggestions from both Christian and secular artists will grab students' attention and prompt meaningful five-minute discussions on critical life topics.

For the music devotions, contact your students to see if you can borrow any of the suggested CDs that aren't a part of your own music library.

To use these movie-clip suggestions, simply set your VCR (or DVD player) to 0:00:00 when the studio logo appears at the beginning of the movie. Then cue the video to the suggested start time, and preview the clip before showing it to students. Also, keep in mind that in general, federal copyright laws do not allow you to use videos (even ones you own) for any purpose other than home viewing. Though some exceptions allow for the use of short segments of copyrighted material for educational purposes, it's best to be on the safe side. Your church can obtain a license from the Motion Picture Licensing Corporation for a small fee. Just visit www.mplc.com or call 1-800-462-8855 for more information.

Topic: Conflict

She Loves Me Not

Scripture Focus: James 4:1-3

Movie: *Shrek* (PG)

Supplies: Bibles, TV, VCR (or DVD player), *Shrek* video (or DVD)

Start Time: 00:35:10 when Shrek starts to stand up.

Stop Time: 00:37:00 when Princess Fiona yells, "But this isn't right!"

Caution!

A swearword is said shortly after this scene in Shrek, *so make sure to end the clip at the recommended stop time.*

The Movie Devotion

Conflict occurs in all relationships. Often it happens when two people's selfish desires bump into each other. In this scene, Shrek saves the princess. His only motive is to make a deal with an evil prince to get his home back. The princess, however, believes that she should be rescued in the proper way. The result is a humorous argument about how the princess should be rescued.

Discussion

• **Why did Shrek and the princess get in an argument? What did each of them want?**

Read James 4:1-3.

• **What causes fights and quarrels?**

• **When have selfish motives caused you to get in a conflict?**

• **What are some practical ways for you to handle conflict?**

• **How can God work in your life as a result of a conflict?**

Topic: Empathy

Jesus Wept

Scripture Focus: John 11:32-36

Movie: Dr. Seuss' *How the Grinch Stole Christmas* (PG)

Supplies: Bibles, TV, VCR (or DVD player), *How the Grinch Stole Christmas* video (or DVD)

Start Time: 00:41:00 when the Grinch says, "Kids today—so desensitized by movies and television."

Stop Time: 43:35 when the Grinch's dog picks up the invitation in his mouth.

The Movie Devotion

The Grinch hates Christmas and all the Whos in Whoville. Cindy Lou Who is a young girl who is having some doubts about Christmas and doesn't share the same excitement as everyone else in town. She decides that the Grinch should be elected the "Holiday Cheer Meister" because he is in the most need of holiday cheer, and she treks up to his mountain cave to personally invite him to the town's Christmas party.

Discussion

• **What did Cindy Lou have in common with the Grinch?**

• **How did she feel about his lack of holiday cheer? How did she treat him?**
Read John 11:32-36.

• **How did Jesus feel about the death of Mary's brother?**

• **How is that like having empathy for someone?**

• **How can having empathy for someone help your relationship with that person?**

Topic: Family

Call Me Crazy!

Scripture Focus: Matthew 10:34-37

Movie: *Rudy* (PG)

Supplies: Bibles, TV, VCR (or DVD player), *Rudy* video (or DVD)

Start Time: 00:21:15 when Rudy is waiting for the bus.

Stop Time: 00:23:50 when Rudy's dad says, "It's not for us."

The Movie Devotion

Caution!

A swearword is said shortly after this scene in Rudy, *so make sure to end the clip at the recommended stop time.*

Rudy is a true story about a young man who followed his dream to play college football despite daunting odds. This scene depicts the conflict he had with his dad about going to college. Rudy is determined to go to Notre Dame, even though he doesn't have good grades and no one in his family has ever gone to college. His father disapproves of his decision, but Rudy decides to go to college against his father's wishes.

Discussion

• How would you describe Rudy's relationship with his dad?

• How do you think that relationship affected him? How do family relationships affect you?

• Did Rudy do the right thing? Is it ever OK to disobey your parents or go against your family's wishes? Explain.

Read Matthew 10:34-37.

• In your own words, what is Jesus saying here?

• How can you balance your commitment to your family with your commitment to follow Jesus?

Topic: Focus on God

Staying Focused

Scripture Focus: Matthew 6:33

Movie: *Chicken Run* (G)

Supplies: Bibles, TV, VCR (or DVD player), *Chicken Run* video (or DVD)

Start Time: 00:16:20 when a chicken closes the drapes and gives a "thumbs up" sign.

Stop Time: 00:18:05 when Ginger walks out the door and it slams behind her.

The Movie Devotion

The chickens on Tweedy's farm have tried to escape many times—but always failed. Ginger, their ringleader, is absolutely determined to escape. In this scene she tries to rally the troops for another escape attempt at a secret henhouse meeting.

Discussion

• When Ginger is determined even at million-to-one odds, do you think she's being brave or foolish? Why?

• What's something you've wanted so badly that you wouldn't quit trying to get or achieve it?

Read Matthew 6:33.

• What kind of focus does this verse describe?

• What would happen if we desired to know and follow God with Ginger's intensity and single-mindedness? How would your life change or stay the same?

• What can you do to improve your focus on following God?

Topic: Forgiveness

Turn the Other Cheek?

Scripture Focus: Matthew 5:38-48

Song: "Hit 'Em Up Style" by Blu Cantrell from the album *So Blu* (2001)

Supplies: Bibles, CD player, *So Blu* CD

The Music Devotion

In "Hit 'Em Up Style," Blu Cantrell sings a song of unforgiveness. Her man has cheated on her, and she wants revenge—big time. Determined to make him pay for what he has done, she goes on a shopping spree, saying goodbye to the good times they had and the hopes and dreams they shared as she listens to the sound of the cash register. Ask students to listen carefully to the lyrics as you play the song "Hit 'Em Up Style."

Discussion

• What is Blu trying to do through her actions? How would she feel afterward?

Read Matthew 5:38-48.

• What advice does Jesus give to someone in Blu's situation? Why should we forgive instead of getting revenge?

• Jesus tells us to show our forgiveness in dramatic ways. What are they?

• Turning the other cheek sounds a bit weak. What effect would this action have on the person who is being aggressive?

• Whose example would you find most difficult to follow: Blu's or Jesus'? Why? Whose example would you choose to follow?

Topic: God's Love

Jesus Loves Me, This I Know

Scripture Focus: 1 John 4:8

Song: "Fallin' " by Alicia Keys from the album *Songs in A Minor* (2001)

Supplies: Bibles, CD player, *Songs in A Minor* CD

The Music Devotion

In this song, Alicia Keys sings about the ups and downs of a romantic relationship. "Fallin' " depicts love as something that changes constantly.

Play the song for your teenagers. Afterward, ask them to name some of the characteristics of romantic love that she sings about. Some of their answers might include "intense," "temporary," "painful," "strong," or "pleasurable." Next, ask your teenagers to think about God's love for us and to compare the characteristics of God's love with the love described in "Fallin'."

> **Discussion**
> • How does God's love differ from romantic love? How does romantic love mirror God's?
> • Does God's love for us have any limits? Explain.
> • Does God fall in and out of love with us? Explain.
> Read 1 John 4:8.
> • How does accepting God's love for you affect your love for others?
> • How can you better reflect God's love in your actions and relationships?

Topic: Gossip

But Words Can Never Hurt Me

Scripture Focus: James 3:5-8

Movie: *Dumbo* (G)

Supplies: Bibles, TV, VCR (or DVD player), *Dumbo* video (or DVD)

Start Time: 00:9:40 when Mrs. Jumbo unwraps her baby.

Stop Time: 00:11:25 when Mrs. Jumbo shuts the door on the female elephants.

The Movie Devotion

Mrs. Jumbo has just received a present from the visiting stork: a brand-new baby. The other female elephants are quick to praise how cute the baby is—until the little pachyderm unfolds his enormous ears. Immediately, the other elephants change their tune, gossiping cruelly about baby Dumbo's appearance.

Discussion

• **What do you think of Mrs. Jumbo's behavior? Was it rude? excusable? praiseworthy? What's your opinion?**

• **Describe a time others were gossiping about you. How did it feel? How did you want to respond?**

• **Respond to this statement: "If others are talking about you, just ignore them." Do you think this is good advice or bad advice? Why?**

Read James 3:5-8.

• **What is it about gossip that seduces us to join in?**

• **Why should we resist the temptation to gossip?**

Topic: Grace

Beauty From Ugliness

Scripture Focus: 2 Corinthians 8:9

Song: "Grace" by U2 from the album *All That You Can't Leave Behind* (2000)

Supplies: Bibles, CD player, *All That You Can't Leave Behind* CD

The Music Devotion

"Grace" is a beautiful song that depicts grace as a person. This idea can help kids think about the incarnation: God's love and grace in human form. Jesus, the ultimate example of God's grace, came to earth as one of us to bring God's love to us. He longs to transform the hurt and pain of sin in our lives. God's grace is similar to an oyster, turning a simple grain of sand into a pearl of great worth. Ask students to close their eyes and listen to the lyrics as you play the song "Grace."

Discussion

• Think for a moment about something you did that was wrong or someone you hurt. What was the consequence of your actions?

Read 2 Corinthians 8:9.

• How and when did Jesus become poor? How has this made us rich?

• How do oysters make pearls? Why is this a good metaphor to use for grace?

• How has God's grace made "beauty out of ugly things" in your life?

Topic: Heaven

Imagining Heaven

Scripture Focus: Revelation 5:11-13

Song: "I Can Only Imagine" by MercyMe from the album *Almost There* (2001)

Supplies: Bibles, CD player, *Almost There* CD

The Music Devotion

"I Can Only Imagine" explores the ideas and feelings that a person might experience when he or she thinks about heaven.

When you begin this devotion, introduce the topic to your students, and ask them to imagine what they might feel when they are in heaven. Then play "I Can Only Imagine" from MercyMe's *Almost There* CD.

Ask students to share what their thoughts about heaven were as they listened to the song. Mention that thinking about heaven can be really uplifting, because as Christians we know that after our physical life is done, heaven will be our eternal home.

Discussion

• What do people who aren't Christians think about heaven?

• What do Christians think about heaven?

Read Revelation 5:11-13.

• How does the passage describe heaven?

• What do you imagine about heaven and what you will do when you get there?

> • How can focusing more on heaven help you as you live your life this week?

Topic: Hell

Cast Out

Scripture Focus: Luke 16:19-31

Movie: *Cast Away* (PG-13)

Supplies: Bibles, TV, VCR (or DVD player), *Cast Away* video (or DVD)

Start Time: 00:36:30 (on video/DVD #1) when Chuck Noland yells, "Hello, anybody!"

Stop Time: 00:38:25 (on video/DVD #1) when Chuck sees the sign that he has written in the sand being washed away.

The Movie Devotion

In this movie, Chuck Noland survives a plane crash and finds himself stranded on a deserted island, totally separated from all contact with civilization. His loneliness eventually causes him to make up an imaginary friend and even to contemplate suicide. In this scene, Chuck begins to experience his separation from the rest of humanity.

Discussion

• What would bother you most about being separated from the rest of the world?

Read Luke 16:19-31.

• How did the rich man experience separation from God?

• What do you imagine hell would be like?

• What is the most frightening thing about hell?

• What warning might the rich man send us?

Topic: Humility

What's So Great About Humility?

Scripture Focus: Proverbs 11:2

Movie: *The Road to El Dorado* (PG)

Supplies: Bibles, TV, VCR (or DVD player), *The Road to El Dorado* video (or DVD)

Start Time: 00:30:42 when Miguel says, "Tulio, we'll be living like kings!"

Stop Time: 00:31:32 when the horse laughs.

Caution!

A swearword is said immediately before this scene, so make sure to cue the clip to the recommended start time.

The Movie Devotion

Two adventurers following a map into the "new world" are mistaken for gods because of their foreign appearance. They realize that if they play the role well, they'll end up rich. If they fail, they're dead.

In this scene, Miguel and Tulio have just been escorted into their palace and think they're alone. They don't realize that their conversation is being overheard.

Discussion

• **Ouch! Our heroes were found out, their real selves revealed. Name a time you were humbled when you said or did something that shattered the image others had of you.**

• **How do you respond when you're humbled? Why?**

Read Proverbs 11:2.

• **Why do you think that with humility comes wisdom?**

• **God clearly wants his followers to be humble. What benefits will come to you—in addition to wisdom—if you choose to be humble rather than prideful?**

Topic: Idolatry

No Other

Scripture Focus: Isaiah 45:18-25

Song: "Nothing Compares" by Third Day from the album *Come Together* (2001)

Supplies: Bibles, CD player, *Come Together* CD

The Music Devotion

"Nothing Compares" explores the many things in life that people seek: glory, good food, riches, and so on. The song concludes that none of these things even compare to knowing God. Use this song to help teenagers consider how their own goals, desires, or interests can become idols in their lives if they supersede their love for God.

The Discussion

Read Isaiah 45:18-25.

• How would you define an idol? What kinds of idols did Israel have?

• What did God want Israel to know about himself?

• What idols do we have today? How did the song we just listened to deal with the subject of idols?

• If God were to speak to us directly right now, what do you think God would say to us about these idols and about himself?

• What would you recognize in your life as idols? How can God help you give him all your love and devotion?

Topic: Jesus' Birth

Right Under Your Nose

Scripture Focus: Luke 2:8-20

Movie: *Men in Black* (PG-13)

Supplies: Bibles, TV, VCR (or DVD player), *Men in Black* video (or DVD)

Start Time: 01:06:30 when K asks the dog about Orion's belt.

Stop Time: 01:08:50 when the woman stares into the galaxy.

The Movie Devotion

Two alien-police have been trying to save the world. They need to find a missing galaxy, and the only clue they have is that it is on "Orion's belt." As it turns out, Orion is a pet cat, the belt is his collar, and the whole galaxy is only about an inch wide. They have missed it all along because they were looking in the wrong place.

Discussion

• **Why was it so hard for them to find the missing galaxy?**

• **Imagine you'd heard that God was coming to earth. What would you have looked for?**

Read Luke 2:8-20.

• **What do you think the shepherds felt and thought when they heard that God had come to earth as a baby?**

• **What about Jesus' birth is surprising?**

• **How has Jesus' birth impacted your life?**

Topic: Leadership

Change the World!

Scripture Focus: Philippians 2:12-16a

Movie: *Casablanca* (PG)

Supplies: Bibles, TV, VCR (or DVD player), *Casablanca* video (or DVD)

Start Time: 00:51:20 when Victor Laszlo and Ilsa enter Captain Renault's office.

Stop Time: 00:54:20 when Victor says, "Good day," and he and Ilsa get up to leave.

The Movie Devotion

In this movie, Victor Laszlo is a leader of the underground movement in Europe fighting to prevent German occupation during World War II. He is a beloved and heroic figurehead among his people and is despised by Hitler's Third Reich. Lazlo had once been imprisoned in a concentration camp and left for dead by the Nazis, who later unhappily discovered he had escaped and was back at work, rallying patriotism among nationals and causing headaches for the Germans. Now Lazlo and his wife Ilsa are running for their lives and have made it to French-occupied Morocco, where the Germans can do little more than threaten them.

In this scene, Major Strasser gives Lazlo an ultimatum: Rat out the leaders of the underground in Europe, or face dire consequences. Of course, Laszlo refuses and gives a stirring speech about the hundreds and thousands who are prepared to take his place if anything happened to him. The Major disagrees, stating that no one would be able to re-place Laszlo.

This short glimpse offers a lot of insight about what made Laszlo an effective leader—courage, a sense of purpose that superseded his own life and well-being, the conviction to fight for what's right, and the ability to inspire others.

Discussion

- **What qualities made Victor Laszlo a standout leader?**
- **How would you describe an especially effective leader?**
- **What character flaws cripple someone's ability to lead others?**

Read Philippians 2:12-16a.

- **What impact do you feel you are having on others?**
- **How can you be a better role model to those who are guided by your behavior?**

Topic: Loneliness

All Dressed Up and No Place to Go

Scripture Focus: Hebrews 13:5

Movie: *Toy Story 2* (G)

Supplies: Bibles, TV, VCR (or DVD player), *Toy Story 2* video (or DVD)

Start Time: 00:08:15 when Andy enters his room.

Stop Time: 00:12:30 when Woody yells, "Yard sale!"

The Movie Devotion

In this clip, Woody, the cowboy, is excited to go to cowboy camp with his owner, Andy. But when his arm gets ripped, he ends up being left behind. As a result of his injury, Woody is "shelved" and feels the sadness and loneliness of someone who has been rejected.

Discussion

• In the movie, what does it mean for a toy when it is "shelved"?

• What might it mean for a person to be "shelved"?

• Describe what it feels like to be lonely. What are some of the emotions that often accompany loneliness?

Read Hebrews 13:5.

• What is God's promise in this passage? What does it mean to you?

• What are some things that we can do to make ourselves aware of God's constant presence when we feel lonely?

Topic: Loyalty

Tried and True

Scripture Focus: Ruth 1:8-17

Song: "At Your Side" by The Corrs from the album *In Blue* (2000)

Supplies: Bibles, CD player, *In Blue* CD

The Music Devotion

Before you play the song "At Your Side," instruct students that as they listen to the song, they should listen for words that have to do with loyalty. Then play the song "At Your Side" from The Corrs' *In Blue* CD. After the song is finished, ask students to share the words about loyalty they remember from the song.

Before you read the Scripture passage, let your students know some background about the context. Explain that it's about Naomi who, after her husband and sons died, encouraged her daughters-in-law to return to their homeland. But one of them decided to stay with Naomi instead.

Discussion

Read Ruth 1:8-17.

- **Why do you think Ruth wanted to stay with Naomi?**
- **How are the song and the Scripture passage similar or different?**
- **How easy or difficult is it to be loyal to someone?**
- **How can you express your loyalty to someone this week?**

Topic: Romance

For the Love of God

Scripture Focus: Ephesians 5:25-27

Song: "God's Romance" by Delirious? from the album *Glo* (2000)

Supplies: Bibles, CD player, *Glo* CD

The Music Devotion

"God's Romance" discusses how God's love for us is like a romance. He loves us with a dedication, purity, and passion that should lead us to thanksgiving and worship.

Before playing the song, invite teenagers to brainstorm words and images that they associate with the idea of romance. Get both girls and guys to give you some ideas of scenarios that they consider especially romantic. Then play the song and lead a discussion.

Discussion

- **What does this song mean when it says that we are "God's romance"?**
- **How do the song's title and content relate to our earlier ideas of romance?**

Read Ephesians 5:25-27.

- **According to this passage, what are some of the characteristics of Christ's love for the church?**
- **How does Christ's love for the church offer a model of truly romantic love?**
- **What principles of Christ's romance for his people can be applied to the way that Christians should treat each other in "romantic" relationships?**

Topic: Secular Music and Movies

Can You Take Me Higher?

Scripture Focus: Psalm 33:1-3

Songs: "Higher" by Creed from the album *Human Clay* (1999) and "Collide" by Jars of Clay from the album *If I Left the Zoo* (1999)

Supplies: Bibles, CD player, *Human Clay* CD and *If I Left the Zoo* CD

The Music Devotion

Play Creed's song "Higher." It's probably a song your teenagers are already familiar with, so ask them to listen specifically for religious themes in the lyrics. After the song is over, have them share any Christian or religious themes they heard. Next play Jars of Clay's "Collide." Ask students to share any Christian themes they heard in this song.

Discussion

• What makes one song fall in the Christian category and the other in the secular category? Do you agree with those assessments?

• Is a song Christian or sacred because of the lyrics, the religious affiliation of the person singing, the way it is sung, or the place in which it is sung? Is it what you feel in your heart while you listen to it? Explain.

Read Psalm 33:1-3.

• What characteristics of music are mentioned here?

• Can your faith be enriched by music that is termed *secular*? What about movies that are secular? Defend your answer.

• Are there kinds of secular music that are not OK to listen to or secular movies that are not OK to watch? If so, how do you draw the line?

Topic: Violence

You're Dead Meat

Scripture Focus: Psalm 11:5

Movie: *A Knight's Tale* (PG-13)

Caution!

Rear nudity is shown in the scene prior to this clip, so make sure to cue the clip to the recommended start time.

Supplies: Bibles, TV, VCR (or DVD player), *A Knight's Tale* video (or DVD)

Start Time: 00:27:30 when Geoffrey says, "Behold my Lord Ulrich."

Stop Time: 00:30:35 when William and the others walk into the marketplace and Geoffrey says, "Do you want to touch him?"

The Movie Devotion

In this scene, William masquerades as Sir Ulrich and wins his first sword-fighting tournament matches. Although the crowd isn't sure what to think of his eloquent friend Geoffrey Chaucer's introduction, they are completely won over by William's style. In the time period in which this movie is set, jousting and sword fighting are the sports of choice. This clip depicts the great appeal they held for the crowd.

Discussion

• Are jousting and sword fighting violent? Why or why not? What about football, basketball, boxing, or wrestling?

• What makes something violent? The intentions of the people involved? The end result? Explain.

• Why do you think some sports fans are attracted to sports that can hurt the competitors?

Read Psalm 11:5.

• Do you think those who love violent sports or violent movies are included in those the Lord hates? Why or why not?

• When, if ever, is violence appropriate?

Topic: Worship

Deserving of Our Praise

Scripture Focus: Colossians 3:16-17

Song: "Stand Here With Me" by Creed from the album *Weathered* (2001)

Supplies: Bibles, CD player, *Weathered* CD

The Music Devotion

The song "Stand Here With Me" can be interpreted as the speaker talking to God (though others may interpret it as depicting a human relationship).

Have teenagers sit and close their eyes while you play the song. As they listen, tell them to pick a word or phrase from the song that might depict their relationships with Jesus, such as "believe," "still fall short," "You're a melody," or "You stand here with me now." After the song, read aloud Colossians 3:16-17, and invite students to reflect quietly on the Scripture. Ask them to think about what worship means.

Say: **Worship is a way for us to strengthen our commitment to God. He loves us unconditionally, he sent us his Son, and in return we honor him with song and prayer. And our commitment can grow even stronger when we worship together.**

Discussion

- **Do any of the lyrics in this song describe your faith? How?**
- **Is this song a worship song? Why or why not?**

Read Colossians 3:16-17.

- **How do you define *worship*?**
- **Are there limits to the way we should worship? If so, what are they?**
- **How can worship enrich your relationship with God? How can you grow in your worship this week?**

Object-Lesson Devotions

*J*esus told stories using seeds, coins, and fish (just to name a few) to communicate truth. Using everyday objects can be a powerful way for you, like Jesus, to help teenagers understand how God's Word applies to their lives. In these object-lesson devotions, you'll discover active, five-minute ideas for using a light bulb, scuba gear, a toaster, a dog leash, and even a frozen turkey to kick-start a meaningful Bible discussion.

Topic: The Bible

Unlocking Answers

Scripture Focus: Psalm 119:9-18

Supplies: Bibles, several padlocks with matching keys as well as many other nonmatching keys.

The Object-Lesson Devotion

Before your students arrive, hide the keys you've gathered all over your meeting room.

Begin by greeting your teenagers and having them form smaller groups of three or four. Give each group a padlock.

Explain that the keys to their padlocks are hidden somewhere in the room. At the cue, students should race to find their hidden keys.

Tell teenagers to begin, and allow them a few minutes to scramble around, trying all of the keys until they find the matching one.

When students have unlocked their padlocks, discuss how many world religions seek to answer life's mysteries. Explain that while many believe that any genuine faith will do, there is only one place where they can find the real answers to their spiritual questions: the Bible.

Discussion

• How was searching for the right key to unlock your padlock similar to searching for truth?

• What is so important about the Bible? Why won't just any religious teachings do?

Read Psalm 119:9-18.

• According to this passage, how can the Bible change one's life? How else can the Bible help you?

• What can you do to be even more influenced by God's Word?

• How can you use the Bible to find answers to your own spiritual questions?

Topic: Divorce

Split Down the Middle

Scripture Focus: Genesis 2:24

Supplies: Bibles, photograph of your mother and photo-graph of your father

The Object-Lesson Devotion

Show the photos to your group. Ask them if they can see what you have inherited from your parents in terms of looks—maybe your nose is like your mom's and your hair is like your dad's. Talk about other things such as hobbies or mannerisms that they have passed on to you. Ask students to talk about what they have inherited from their parents.

Sensitivity Required

As you discuss this topic, be sensitive to students whose parents are divorced. Invite them to share their feelings, but also respect their privacy.

Explain that although we inherit some things from our moms and some from our dads, each of us is a unique, single person that can't be split into two! Ask students how this compares to the oneness God has designed for marriage.

Discussion

Read Genesis 2:24.

• What does God say happens when two people get married? What do you think this means?

• How does becoming "one flesh" affect the way a couple makes decisions, relates to their friends, or plans their future?

• What did God intend for marriage? What happens to the "one flesh" unit when a couple separates or gets divorced?

• God is gracious and can heal and restore broken people. What should Christians do if their marriages are in difficulty?

• What is your dream regarding marriage and your future?

Topic: Faith

Seeing Is Believing... Sometimes

Scripture Focus: John 20:24-29

Supplies: Bibles, small rubber ball, 3 identical plastic cups (that aren't transparent)

The Object-Lesson Devotion

You might want to practice this trick at home a few times. It will work better if you use short, heavier cups.

Share the Fun!

If you have time, invite some teenagers to also demonstrate the trick for the rest of the students.

Turn the three cups upside down on a smooth surface, and place the ball under one of the cups. Tell the students to try to keep their eyes on the cup with the ball in it. Rotate the three cups as fast as you can; the longer you keep them moving, the likelier it is that your audience will lose track of the cup with the ball in it. When students' eyes start to glaze over, stop and ask everyone which cup is holding the ball. Then reveal to them which cup the ball is really under.

Discussion

• What are some similarities between this game and our faith?

• Do you think we're encouraged to trust our eyes in life more than our other senses, instincts, and emotions? If so, why?

Read John 20:24-29.

- Would you have been like Thomas, asking to see with your eyes? Why or why not?
- Why are those "who have not seen and yet have believed" blessed? What does this say about faith?
- In what matters of faith do you need to work on believing what you cannot see?

Topic: The Future

Tomorrow and Tomorrow and Tomorrow

Scripture Focus: Jeremiah 29:11

Supplies: Bibles, calendar that contains the dates for the next several months or years

The Object-Lesson Devotion

Help your teenagers begin thinking about the future by holding up a calendar for the year or one that contains the dates for the next several years. Flip through it a bit, showing the pictures inside and inviting students to declare the months of their birthdays. Then give students a date several months or several years in the future, and ask for the correct day of the week (for example, "February 22, 2005 is what day of the week?"). After doing this for several different dates, lead a discussion.

Discussion
- Why do so many people keep calendars and personal schedule books?
- Can a person really plan for his or her future? Defend your answer.
- What hopes and fears do you have when you think about your future? Read Jeremiah 29:11.
- What does this passage tell us about God's plan for the future of his people? How does this apply to your own life?
- How can you live differently knowing that God has a plan for your future?

Handle With Care

Scripture Focus: Philippians 4:5

Supplies: Bibles, 2 new light bulbs, 1 "burnt-out" light bulb with a broken filament, lamp (without a light bulb)

The Object-Lesson Devotion

Have teenagers stand in a circle (at least ten feet in diameter), and give them a new light bulb. Instruct them to gently throw the light bulb around the circle without breaking it. The catch? They cannot toss it to someone next to them, and they can only throw it to someone who hasn't had it yet. Once they make it around, have them try it a few more times.

After the game, have teenagers gather around the lamp as you first screw in a new light bulb and demonstrate that it works by turning the lamp on, and then as you screw in their light bulb to see if it still works. (If teenagers have actually broken the glass of their light bulb, simply skip this part of the demonstration.) It is possible that tossing the bulb around may have dislodged the filament so that the bulb will not light up. Finally, screw in the burnt-out light bulb, and demonstrate that it doesn't work.

Explain that even though the exterior of the burnt-out light bulb looks fine, the filament on the inside is very fragile and is easily broken. Say: **Being gentle with a light bulb means more than just trying not to break the glass. It means handling the bulb very carefully so that even the small, fragile parts on the inside aren't damaged.**

Shake It Up, Baby!

For this lesson you'll need one light bulb that doesn't have broken glass but is "burnt-out." You can use one from your home that doesn't work anymore, or you can shake a new light bulb until the filament is broken and it will no longer work.

Discussion

• How is the gentle treatment required for handling a light bulb similar to the way we should treat people? How is it different?

• Why might the sign "Handle With Care" appropriately be placed over our hearts and souls?

Read Philippians 4:5.

• What does it mean to be a "gentle" person?

• Would you consider it a compliment to be called gentle? (Be honest!) Why or why not?

• How can you show gentleness to others this week?

Topic: Gifts and Talents

All for One

Scripture Focus: Romans 12:3-8

Supplies: Bibles, toaster, newsprint, marker, tape,

The Object-Lesson Devotion

Tape a sheet of newsprint in a prominent location, and draw a line down the middle of the paper. Also, set out the toaster.

Have students pass around the toaster as each person examines it and all of its parts. While they're doing that, have them brainstorm the different people or jobs needed to make a toaster and get it into a person's home. (Possible ideas may be an electrician, an engineer, a designer, a salesperson, a marketer to create ad campaigns, and a delivery person to distribute the toasters.) Write their ideas on the left side of the newsprint.

Talk about how, in order to get a toaster into our homes, many different skills are required. In the same way, God needs people with different abilities and talents in order to do his work.

Next, ask students to think of abilities and skills teenagers have that they can use to do God's work. List these on the right side of the newsprint.

Read Romans 12:3-8 and then use the following questions to guide your discussion.

Discussion

• How can our different talents and spiritual gifts work together to accomplish God's work?

• Are any gifts more important than others? Explain your answer.

• What should our reason be for using our gifts?

• How do our different gifts unify us?

Topic: Greed

Unstoppable

Scripture Focus: Luke 12:13-21, 32-34

Supplies: Bibles, perpetual-motion toy with swinging balls

The Object-Lesson Devotion

Ask volunteers to get the perpetual-motion toy moving for as short a time as possible. Tell students you want the balls to stop moving on their own without anyone physically touching  the toy. Have the volunteers touch only an end ball, pulling it back and softly letting it go. Allow three or four students to set the toy in motion. Make sure each teenager who starts the toy's motion slightly increases the distance from which the first ball is let go. (This will make it even more difficult for the motion to be stopped.)

The Discussion

Read Luke 12:13-21, 32-34.

• What do these verses say about greed?

• Compare greed to this perpetual-motion toy. How can one small desire for something be like the ball that's first dropped?

• Does the pattern of greed stop on its own? Explain.

• What kinds of things are we sometimes greedy for? What does Jesus say we should desire instead?

• How do you think we can begin desiring the things that are good for us—the things God wants to satisfy us with?

Topic: Holiness

Clouding the Issue

Scripture Focus: Romans 12:1-2

Supplies: Bibles, large glass filled with water, dark shade of food coloring (such as blue or green), index card, marker

The Object-Lesson Devotion

Before you begin, write the word *Jesus* on the index card in regular-sized handwriting.

Start by explaining to teenagers that God wants their lives to be as pure as the water in front of them. Put the index card behind the glass, and ask a student to read aloud what the card says. Share with students that holiness in their lives will allow others to see Jesus through them.

Now invite students one at a time to add just a drop of food coloring to the water. Once the water is sufficiently cloudy, hold the card behind the glass again, and explain that just a little sin can cloud their whole lives, making it harder for others to see Jesus through them.

Discussion

• **What does it look like when sin clouds your life? What are some examples?**

Read Romans 12:1-2.

• **What does it mean to be a living sacrifice? Explain it in your own words.**

• **What does a holy life look like? Give examples.**

• **Why is living a holy life difficult?**

• **How can you personally grow in holiness?**

Topic: The Holy Spirit

Breath of God

Scripture Focus: Acts 2:2

Supplies: Bibles, electric fan

The Object-Lesson Devotion

Mood Music

Try to set a contemplative mood for the experience by playing soft music in the background.

Have students stand in front of a fan, one by one. Ask them to close their eyes and imagine the blowing air as the Holy Spirit touching their bodies. Ask them to think about what the Holy Spirit is trying to tell them at this point in their lives.

Discussion
• **What are some of the characteristics of wind?**

Read Acts 2:2.

• **Why is the Holy Spirit compared to wind and to breath?**

• **When is the Spirit a violent, rushing wind, and when is it gentle like breath?**

• **Have you ever felt the presence of the Holy Spirit in your life? What was that experience like?**

• **How can you better listen to the Holy Spirit?**

Topic: Jesus' Death

The Lifeline

Scripture Focus: Luke 23:39-43

Supplies: Bibles, scuba gear

The Object-Lesson Devotion

Not a Diver?

If you don't have scuba diving experience, invite a diver from your church or community to help out with this devotion and explain the functions of the various pieces of equipment.

Display scuba gear to the group. Ask a student to volunteer to try it on while you explain how it works.

Explain to the teenagers that air is delivered from the air tanks on the diver's back, through the air hose, to the mouthpiece. The air hose is literally a lifeline keeping the diver alive. If the air hose were cut while someone was diving, he or she would not be able to breathe.

However, if two divers are diving and the air hose on one of the tanks gets damaged, the diver might not die. The second diver can save the first by passing the mouthpiece with the good air hose back and forth between them. Only if someone substitutes a good air hose for a bad one can the diver live.

Say: **When we sin, we cut ourselves off from God, the source of life. It's like we cut our own air hose. But Jesus never sinned; he never cut the air hose, or his** connection to God. So Jesus decided to save us by giving us his good life in exchange for our lives that have been damaged by sin. On the cross, he took our sins on himself.

Discussion

• Sin cuts us off from God, the source of life. How have you experienced this disconnection in your own life?

Read Luke 23:39-43.

• How did Jesus restore the thief's connection to God? How do you think the thief felt when he spoke with Jesus?

• How did Jesus switch air hoses with us and reconnect us to God? Explain it in your own words.

• What does Jesus' death mean to you?

Topic: Joy

Deep Within

Scripture Focus: 1 Peter 1:8-9

Supplies: Bibles, 1 chocolate peanut butter cup for each student

The Object-Lesson Devotion

Distribute chocolate peanut butter cups. Invite students to unwrap them and then describe them simply based on what they see and smell. Encourage them to pretend they've never seen nor eaten one before and to make very basic observations. Next, ask students to take a bite and then add or change things from their earlier descriptions.

Allergies?

Some people are seriously allergic to peanuts, so make sure you check with your students (or their parents) before doing this activity.

Say: **Though you couldn't see it at first, this snack was filled with peanut butter. The peanut butter flavor makes this snack a lot different from just a regular piece of chocolate.**

Like this snack, Christians are also filled with something special deep within: joy. Though it isn't always visible, the joy of Christ inside makes Christians unique.

Discussion

• When is joy hidden from others? When is it obvious to others? Give examples.

• What's the difference between joy and happiness?

• Is joy an emotion? If not, what is it? How would you define true joy?

Read 1 Peter 1:8-9.

• What is the source of joy in your life? Explain.

• How can joy in Christ sustain you, even through the tough moments of life?

Topic: Kindness

What Are You Wearing?

Scripture Focus: Colossians 3:12-14

Supplies: Bibles, someone else's clothes

The Object-Lesson Devotion

Arrive at the session wearing someone else's clothes. Choose someone who has very different taste in clothing from you or someone who is a different size so that the clothes obviously don't fit. See if students comment on your clothes. If they don't, ask them if they like your new outfit. Start them talking about what they are wearing and how they decided what to put on that morning when they first got out of bed.

Discussion

• Why do you choose the particular style of clothes that you wear?

• What does it feel like to wear someone else's clothes or things that don't fit properly?

Read Colossians 3:12-14.

• What does Paul tell us to clothe ourselves with? Why?

• How can we "put on" kindness? What do we need to do so that we feel comfortable wearing kindness?

• What kind things can you do this week to help you get used to wearing kindness? Who do you most need to be kind to?

Topic: Lust

The Thirst Quencher

Scripture Focus: James 1:13-15

Supplies: Bibles, specialty coffee drink (or a highly caffeinated soda)

The Object-Lesson Devotion

Display a specialty coffee drink (or a highly caffeinated soda) in front of the group. Have a student volunteer drink it and comment on whether or not it quenches his or her thirst.

Say: **Sometimes when you're really thirsty, you'll buy yourself a big, cold soda from the store down the street or a nice, warm espresso drink from your favorite coffee shop. The problem is that the drink actually tricks you. The caffeine in it is a diuretic, which means it dries out your body instead of really satisfying your thirst. If you drink a lot of caffeine, your body ends up thirstier than when you started.**

Explain to students that humans have a deep thirst for sexual satisfaction. When that desire falls outside of God's plans for our sexuality, it is called lust. Lust works like caffeine: The more you try to satisfy it, the thirstier you become. God has designed sex to be satisfying, but not when lust takes over.

Discussion

• **Does lust leave you feeling satisfied? Why or why not?**

Read James 1:13-15.

• **How can desire lead to sin?**

• **Does God care about our physical desires? Explain your answer.**

• **What can help prevent you from seeking false satisfaction for your sexual thirst?**

• **In terms of sexual desire, how can our thirst really be satisfied?**

Topic: Parents

How Long a Leash?

Scripture Focus: Deuteronomy 8:5-6

Supplies: Bibles, retractable dog leash and collar

The Object-Lesson Devotion

With the help of a student, demonstrate how the retractable dog leash works. Don't actually put the collar on the student. Allow as many students as possible to hold the leash and try pulling it out and then allowing it to retract.

Say: **This leash stretches from a few inches to** [fill in the length]. **If a dog gets in trouble when the leash is extended, the owner can shorten it quickly.**

Many teenagers describe their life at home with parents as a life on a leash. Curfews, allowances, rules about dress and activities: They're all set at a certain length that can be instantly lengthened or shortened.

Discussion

• How long would you say your "leash" is at home? How long should it be?

• Generally speaking, are the parents of your friends too permissive or too strict? Explain.

Read Deuteronomy 8:5-6.

• If parents take this seriously, how does that affect "leash length" in their homes?

• What's one thing about "leash length" that you vow you'll remember when you have teenagers of your own?

• How can you demonstrate respect for the limits your parents have set for you?

Topic: Purity

Living by the Truth

Scripture Focus: 1 John 1:5-10

Supplies: Bibles, cassette recorder with microphone, blank cassette tape

The Object-Lesson Devotion

Have teenagers sit in a circle, and set the cassette recorder to "record." Pass around the recorder, and ask everyone to say one word, phrase, or name that reflects something wrong they've done in the past. When everyone has finished, read aloud 1 John 1:5-10. Hold up the recorder.

Say: **Through Jesus, our unrighteousness is erased. Just as we can erase and record on this recorder, we can be purified when we ask for forgiveness. Jesus' love gives us the opportunity to "erase our tapes" and begin a new recording of our life with God.**

As you rewind the tape, ask everyone to pray silently for forgiveness. Then pass the recorder around again, and ask teenagers to take turns reading segments of 1 John 1:5-10.

Discussion
- **How would you define the word *purity*?**
- **How is rerecording on the tape recorder like being purified of sin?**
- **Does being purified change the way you feel about the wrong things you did? Why or why not?**
- **How does Jesus' forgiveness help you with your faith walk?**
- **How do you know when you have to "erase" and "rerecord" in your life?**

Topic: Racism

Red and Yellow, Black and White

Scripture Focus: Galatians 3:26-28

Supplies: Bibles, baseball, highlighter (pink, yellow, or green), paper bag

Open Up the Floor

Discussion of this topic may elicit strong emotions in students, especially those who may have been victims of racial discrimination. If time allows, invite those students who are willing to share some of their experiences and emotions. Use this devotion as an opportunity to start an ongoing dialogue in your student ministry on racism.

The Object-Lesson Devotion

Before students arrive, completely color a baseball with a pink, green, or yellow highlighter. Place the baseball in a deep paper bag that will allow students to reach in and feel the baseball without seeing it.

After students arrive, say: **I want to pass around this bag with a common object inside. When the bag comes to you, reach inside, feel what's there, and offer a one-word description of what's inside—*without* naming the object or looking inside the bag.**

One-word descriptors might include *hard, round, light,* or *seamed.* The color of the ball won't be mentioned because no one can see it.

After the bag has been passed around to everyone, lift the baseball from the bag, and show it to your students.

Discussion

• **Why did you pick the word you chose to describe the baseball?**

• **Had we been able to see the baseball rather than just feel it, do you think the color of the ball would have been used to describe it? Why?**

• **When you're describing someone, do you ever mention the race of the person? Why or why not?**

• **Is racism a problem in the church? Explain your answer.**

Read Galatians 3:26-28.

• **What does this verse say about racial distinctions? How do you need to apply this verse in your daily life?**

Topic: Siblings

Pretzel People

Scripture Focus: Psalm 133:1

Supplies: Bibles, different kinds of "curly" pretzels (not sticks), bowl, paper towels

The Object-Lesson Devotion

Put the pretzels in a bowl, and set out a paper towel for each student.

Have students take as many pretzels as they have siblings, plus one for themselves. Encour-  age them to take different kinds of pretzels so they don't all look alike. (Students who don't have siblings can pair up.)

Have students think of something they have in common with their siblings. (Those without siblings can think of something they have in common with their partners.) Talk about how their pretzels are different, except that they're all pretzels. In the same way, we aren't exactly like our siblings, but we have at least one thing in common with them. And whether or not we have siblings in our immediate families, we also have spiritual siblings in our spiritual families.

Have each student take a small bite out of each pretzel and link the pretzels together so that they are linked together in a circle.

Discussion

• **How are you united with your brothers and sisters? How about your spiritual siblings?**

Read Psalm 133:1.

• **Why is it important to be united?**

• **Why is it difficult sometimes to get along with siblings?**

• **Do arguments and disagreements help or hurt our unity? Explain your answer.**

• **What's one way you can improve your relationship with your siblings?**

Topic: Stress

At the Bursting Point

Scripture Focus: Psalm 94:19

Supplies: Bibles, 1 balloon and 1 thumbtack or safety pin for every 2 people

The Object-Lesson Devotion

Ask teenagers to form pairs, and give each pair a balloon. Explain that one partner should list aloud anything in his or her life that causes stress, such as college admission tests, parents, dating, and sports. For every item named, the other partner should blow a little more air into the balloon. Some pairs will list so many things that the balloon will actually burst. Others may elect to stop before that happens. When all of the groups have exhausted their ideas, distribute thumbtacks to the groups that still have intact balloons, and tell them to pop the balloons, symbolically releasing their stresses.

Discussion

- **Do you ever feel like you're going to explode from stress? If so, when?**
- **What are the major stress factors in your life?**
- **How do you deal with them?**

Read Psalm 94:19.

- **Does God want you to be stressed out? Why or why not?**
- **How can you give your stress to God and enjoy God's consolation this week?**

Topic: Thankfulness

Guest of Honor

Scripture Focus: Ephesians 5:20

Supplies: Bibles, frozen turkey

The Object-Lesson Devotion

Introduce your students to a frozen turkey.

Say: **In America, every November the turkey becomes the symbol of the national holiday of Thanksgiving. When Americans see turkeys, they are moved to consider all the blessings in their lives.**

Unfortunately, the turkeys have a little less to be thankful about.

The name of this particular turkey is Henry. Let's take turns telling our little friend why he should be thankful.

If students are uncomfortable with being put on the spot to supply an answer, instead hold Henry up and indicate that students should call out suggestions.

Suggestions might include "Henry no longer has to worry about losing his head in a crisis," or "Henry's able to keep his cool no matter what."

Discussion

• **How do you feel when you're facing a difficult situation—as Henry clearly has—and people suggest you should be thankful? What do you say?**

• **Describe a time something that appeared to be awful was in reality a blessing from God. What happened?**

• **If God cares so much for us, why does he let painful things happen to us at all?**

Read Ephesians 5:20.

• **What's hard about complying with this directive? What's easy about it?**

• **How can you exercise this principle this week?**

Topic: The Trinity

The Whole Package

Scripture Focus: 2 Corinthians 13:14

Supplies: Bibles, portable CD player with headphones, CD

The Object-Lesson Devotion

Set out the CD player, headphones (not connected to the CD player), and CD. Tell students that the three items illustrate a kind of difficult spiritual truth, and ask them if they know what it is or want to take a guess.

Talk about how the three items by themselves are all different from each other and they do different things. Then connect the headphones to the CD player and put in the CD, and talk about how together they work for one purpose, so we can hear the music. Discuss how that's similar to the Trinity. God, Jesus, and the Holy Spirit are all separate parts of the Trinity, but at the same time they're all God, and they function together as one.

Discussion

• How do you think the CD player and its parts are similar to the Trinity? How is it different from the Trinity?

• What are other objects or examples we're familiar with that can help others better understand the Trinity?

• Why is the Trinity is so hard to understand?

Read 2 Corinthians 13:14.

• What part of the Trinity would you like to know more about, and why?

Topical Index

Scripture Index

Index of Themes Arranged by
Devotion Type

Activity Devotions

Event and Location Devotions

Illustration Devotions

Index of Themes Arranged by
Devotion Type (continued)

Movie and Music Devotions

Object-Lesson Devotions

Index of Locations or Events Used in Devotions

Index of Movies
Used in Devotions

Index of Songs
Used in Devotions

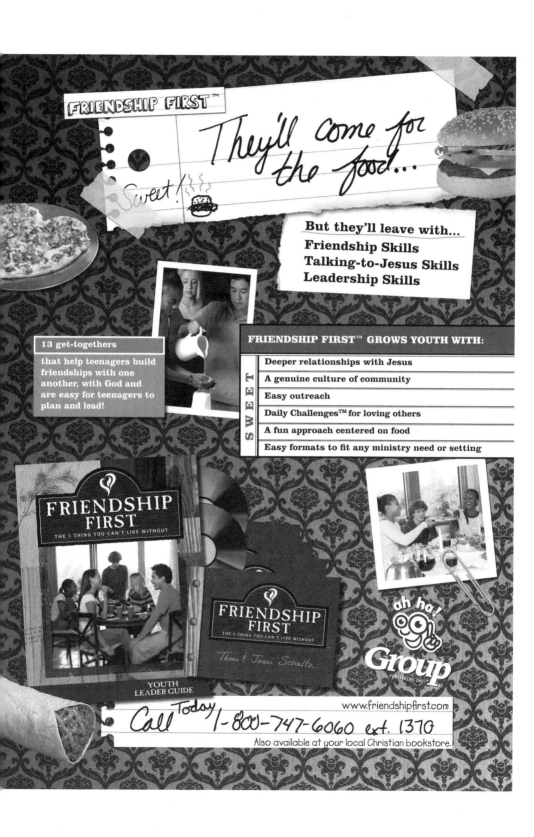

Senior High Books

- Applying God's Word
- Believing in Jesus
- Christian Character
- Family Matters
- Following Jesus
- Is There Life After High School?
- Prayer
- Sexuality
- Sharing Your Faith
- Worshipping 24/7
- Your Christian ID
- Your Relationships

Junior High Books

- Becoming a Christian
- Choosing Wisely
- Fighting Temptation
- Finding Your Identity
- Friends
- God's Purpose for Me
- How to Pray
- My Family Life
- My Life as a Christian
- Sharing Jesus
- Understanding the Bible
- Who Is God?

Preteen Books

- Being Responsible
- Building Friendships
- Getting Along With Other
- God in My Life
- Going Through Tough Tim
- Handling Conflict
- How to Make Great Choic
- Peer Pressure
- Succeeding in School
- The Bible and Me
- What's a Christian?
- Why God Made Me

The Youth Bible

The Bible to use with Faith 4 Life.

Visit your local Christian bookstore,
or contact Group Publishing, Inc., at 800-447-1070.
www.grouppublishing.com